EVERY WOMAN REMEMBERED

Daughters of Newport in the Great War

Sylvia Mason

Published by Saron Publishing in 2018

ISBN-13: 978-0-9956495-2-1

Saron Publishers
Pwllmeyrick House
Mamhilad
Mon
NP4 8RG

www.saronpublishers.co.uk
info@saronpublishers.co.uk
Follow us on Facebook and Twitter

We are grateful to the British Red Cross for permission to use the front cover photo. These three unknown VAD nurses lived in Newport and the photo was taken at St Paul's Church. If anyone has any information as to who they were, the Red Cross would love to hear from you.

Saron Publishers would also like to hear from anyone who knows of any other women who should be included in any future edition of this book.

All of the author's profits and 40% of the publisher's proceeds are being donated to the Newport Women's Bursary, to enable the continuation of the work started by the courageous women whose stories are chronicled in this book.

DEDICATION

To the women of Newport

CONTENTS

ACKNOWLEGEMENTS

Firstly I would like to thank my husband, Colin, who has always supported me.

I would also like to thank Jeanette Hawrot who was in at the start of this project and then Gail Giles who helped me to define the task. Next came Tony Hopkins, County Archivist and manager of Gwent Archives, whose encouragement was a great motivator. He introduced me to Peter Strong, editor of the *Gwent Local History Journal*, whose practical advice I found invaluable. The staff at Gwent Archives were helpful, particularly on one occasion when Monty Dart and I waded through mountains of old school records. The staff of Newport Reference Library have also been generous with their time and help.

The clergy and staff of St John the Evangelist, Maindee, went out of their way to help me. My friend, Ann Hopkins, loaned me books from her extensive collection. Jayne Bryant allowed me to use her Ancestry account until I had my own, and Eira Williams allowed me to use her late husband, Derek's, research on Beatrice White. The following people answered my plea for information in the *Argus*: Shaun McGuire, Mary Walker, Monty Dart and Arthur Roper. All offered positive help and encouragement.

Nigel Young, who runs the Newport Past website, gave permission to use the photographs and family history of his grandmother, Evelyn Ellis. He also supplied me with some old photographs of Newport. He introduced me to Michael Wilkinson who gave me permission to use the photographs of his grandmother and his great aunt, Ethel and Susie Davies. P Burraston, a descendant of Caroline Edwards' sister, Mabel, gave his permission to use the photographs of Caroline and her parents, Evan and Erena. Melodie Neal, who lives in Australia, gave me permission to use the photographs, autograph book and family history of her grandmother, Minnie Sanders. Marie Skinner, who is the granddaughter of Florence and Harry Riding, spoke to me about her memories of Florence and gave her permission to use the diary and photograph.

Throughout, I have received support from Rosemary Butler, who is the founder and chair of the Newport Women's Bursary.

By no means least, many thanks to Penny Reeves of Saron Publishers for all her practical help and, more importantly, for giving me the confidence to believe my work could be published. She made the process a pleasure.

Sylvia Mason
November 2017

Foreword

How would the women who walked Newport's streets in the years before the 1914-1918 War react if they were able to see how their granddaughters and great granddaughters live now? I'm sure they would be enormously heartened to find that so much has changed for the better. Although complete equality of opportunity has yet to be won, it is now recognised that women are capable of filling the most senior positions in public life and can contribute insights that were missing in previously male-dominated decision-making circles. Everyone benefits from the fact that one of the city's two MPs and one of our two Assembly Members are women. Even the Leader of Newport City Council is a woman and she has recently been elected to the highly important position of Chair of the Wales Local Government Association.

By far the biggest impetus for the improved opportunities now available to women was the horrifying and catastrophic war into which Britain and much of the world was drawn in 1914. So many young men lost their lives on the battlefields that women were required to contribute to the war effort, or needed to earn a living following the death of the family's male wage earner. In Newport, women joined the workforce in the Royal Gwent and other local hospitals, drove buses, acted as police officers and postal workers, and even undertook the making of munitions at the National Shell Factory at Maesglas; the kind of jobs that had previously been done by men. In their hundreds of thousands, women threw off the pinafores of domestic service to take up better paid and less subservient forms of employment - and they found the experience liberating. As the war dragged on and the resulting death toll soared ever higher, some of the more courageous joined the Armed Services or volunteered to serve in other capacities close to the mud- and blood-filled trenches. Inevitably, some of them perished.

To mark the centenary of the ending of the First World War, Sylvia Mason has undertaken research into the Newport women who lost their lives alongside their menfolk. Her starting point was the Roll of Honour in Newport Reference Library which lists the city's war dead and she discovered that the list, compiled five years after the war's end, is far from complete. Four women's names are listed but Sylvia's research has uncovered others who also, by right, should be included. She details the lives of seven women and the circumstances in which they met their deaths, either as a result of the dangerous military conditions in which they served or from the illnesses that decimated the wounded soldiers and the nurses who cared for them.

The debt we owe these courageous Newport women, Caroline Edwards, Lilian Jones, Alice Guy, Gertrude Dyer, Frances Llewellyn-Jones, Beatrice White and Violet Phillips, is immense. In this book, Sylvia shows how their sacrifices had long-lasting effects from which we all benefit today.

Without the contribution made by women such as these, Britain would not have emerged victorious. They had helped win the war and, by doing so, proved that women had the right to a political role while remaining mothers and wives. Many reasonable people understood that the pre-war patriarchal society could not, and should not, be re-established. But it needed the brave campaigns, led by the women's suffrage movement, to change public attitudes formed from centuries-old prejudices. In the book, Sylvia also tells us about the leaders of the several suffragette movements in Newport, women such as Margaret Mackworth and Mabel Vivian, who, as part of a nationwide drive, eventually forced the government to give women what they were owed; the vote, the opportunity to stand for Parliament, many previously-lacking rights in law, equality and due respect.

After reading this book, I felt intensely proud of these magnificent Newport women of whom I knew little beforehand. Sylvia must be congratulated for undertaking such a worthwhile project.

I wish to add that Sylvia is generously donating the proceeds from the sales of the book towards the annual Newport Women's Bursary.

The Bursary's purpose is to award funds that will help women fulfil their ambitions. Women aged 18 and over, and who live in Newport, are encouraged to apply for a grant of up to £1000; applications can be made by individuals or groups. All applications are considered by an independent panel and must demonstrate that the money will make a significant difference to the applicant's life. There have been many worthy recipients in the past and the author's extremely generous offer will help ensure more women will have the opportunity to benefit from the Bursary in the future.

Dame Rosemary Butler
Chair, Newport Women's Bursary
December 2017
www.newportwf.wordpress.com
newportwomensforum@live.co.uk

INTRODUCTION

Looking back on old, sepia photographs of Newport taken before World War One, the town looks impossibly distant. It seems, in many ways, to be a different place. Many of the beautiful buildings, recently erected then, are still with us, but the awnings on the shops, the horses, carts and trams in the shopping streets, the women in floor length clothes and statement hats, speak of long lost days.

Pre-war Commercial Street, showing the Clock Tower of the old Town Hall © Newport Reference Library

They were days in which Newport was thriving and prosperous. The population, which was 83,981 in 1911, was growing fast. People were moving into Newport to be part of the opportunities the thriving economy provided. The electric trams, which had recently replaced the horse-drawn trams, were frequent and busy. At the main railway station on High Street, three hundred trains arrived and departed daily. The express train to London took two and a half hours. The newly expanded docks were in their heyday, exporting coal, steel and tinplate. Newport was an international trading centre, busy and self-confident.

Commercial Street c1910 with the Westgate Hotel on the right
© *Newport Reference Library*

The Royal Gwent Hospital (RGH) opened in 1901 with one hundred and ten beds for adults and children, gaining the title 'Royal' in 1913. Long before the National Health Service, the hospital was supported entirely by voluntary contributions. A workhouse, Woolaston House, on Stow Hill (now St Woolos Hospital), was capable of accommodating over six hundred men and women of all ages, although it did not often have this many. It was governed by a Board of Guardians, an elected body which included women.

Pre-war High Street © *Nigel Young*

The main post office on High Street, built in 1907, was open for business six days a week from 7am to 10pm and for two hours on Sunday mornings. The telegraph and telephone departments were on the second floor.

There were a number of fee-paying schools, some with boarding facilities, which catered for all ages. There were also twenty elementary schools and, for brighter, older children, the boys' and the girls' intermediate schools (later Newport High School for Boys and Newport High School for Girls).

Newport had eight public halls available for meetings, some of which could hold up to two thousand people. There were a number of thriving theatres and music halls but, by 1914, these were outnumbered by cinemas and picture houses, including the exotically named, Electric Palace at 99, Commercial Road, and the Empire Palace of Varieties in Charles Street. There were pubs, hotels, restaurants and tearooms, of course.

Pre-war Commercial Road © *Nigel Young*

The social life was teeming. Organisations abounded. Newport had nearly seventy churches of all denominations. Public worship on Sundays was an accepted part of most people's lives, children were routinely baptised and the clergyman was a known and respected member of the social hierarchy. Newport was also a centre of temperance activities. There were no fewer than six temperance societies in the town. The Young Men's Christian Association (YMCA) was in Commercial Street and the Young Women's Christian Association (YWCA) in Palmyra Place. The buildings were used for educational as well as Christian activities.

It was a time when people knew their place, their God-given station in life. The men and women moved along their separate grooves, socialising with people of their own class, and choosing lifestyles considered appropriate for their gender. Middle class women were not expected to be too highly educated, for their role was to marry and run a home. Their domestic servants did the housework, child-care and cooking and were generally at every-one's beck and call. Working class women, apart from those who were domestic servants, often worked outside the home in mills, factories, shops and laundries. All classes placed restrictions on young women. Middle and upper class girls were not allowed out without a chaperone. Respectable working class parents expected good behaviour of their daughters at all times. Society's ideal young woman was a mild, biddable maiden. The poor were the bottom of the heap in this pre-welfare society, and poor women and children the least fortunate of all.

In Newport, the Labour Party was an emerging force but had not yet achieved electoral success. The parliamentary seat of Monmouth Boroughs, (Newport, Monmouth and Usk) was a marginal seat which, before and during World War One, returned a Liberal, Lewis Haslam to Parliament. All political parties had their parallel or auxiliary women's organisations. The women raised funds and helped to get the male representatives elected. For many women, this was not enough and Newport was buzzing with women's political activity. For years, a large number of women and some men had been arguing for equal suffrage.

Possibly the most famous suffragette in Wales, Margaret Haig Thomas, at that time known as Lady Margaret Mackworth, lived in Newport. Her father was the millionaire coal owner and ex-Liberal MP David Alfred Thomas. Her mother, Sybil Haig Thomas, was a feminist, an active campaigner for women's suffrage, and president of the pro-suffrage Welsh Union of

Women's Liberal Associations. They lived in Llanwern Park House, now demolished. From 1908, Margaret Mackworth was secretary of the Newport Branch of the Women's Social and Political Union (WSPU). This group consisted of militants who worked vociferously in support of votes for women.

The National Union of Women's Suffrage Societies (NUWSS) which, nationally, had almost ten times as many members as the WSPU, was the other main pro-suffrage group. In Newport, its chair was Mabel Vivian, head-mistress of the Girls Intermediate School. Members worked to achieve their aims in a peaceful and law-abiding way, but naturally this attracted far less publicity. Alongside these two, and some smaller pro-suffrage groups, there was the Newport branch of the National League for Opposing Women's Suffrage. They were known as 'the antis'. This group was well-supported and very active.

In Newport, these groups held large meetings and rallies, raised funds, produced leaflets, had stalls and shops on Commercial Street and knocked doors to stimulate support. They lobbied everyone who had any influence. Their meetings and activities were reported at length in the local newspapers. Female suffrage was an issue which the citizens of Newport could not ignore - until it was eclipsed by war.

The Great War was started by actions far away in Bosnia but what triggered Britain's entry into the conflict on 4th August 1914, was Germany's invasion of Belgium. Wars previously had caused shock and bereavement, but nothing prepared the people of Newport for the impact of this war. At the start, newspapers were prevented by the Defence of the Realm Act, enacted four days after the start of the war, from printing anything which could assist the enemy or cause unhappiness at home. The ban on journalists going to the front and writing about it proved to be unworkable but most were staunchly patriotic so they trumpeted battles won and downplayed battles lost. When, in August 1916, the film *The Battle of the Somme* did the rounds of the cinemas, people queued around the block to see it, but again it was staunchly patriotic. A great deal of the horror had been cut, as the War Office did not want to lose public support for the war. Letters from the front were censored. What must have shockingly brought the reality home was the lengthening casualty lists in the papers. The *Weekly Argus* printed pictures, names and addresses whenever possible.

My father was a schoolboy in Cardiff during the war, too young to enlist but old enough to read the papers with the growing lists of the dead. He was about to start his secondary education in Howard Gardens School when war was declared and it was decided to use this building for wounded soldiers, so the boys occupied the infants department of Crwys Road School. He remembered walking to school and seeing in nearly every front window a sign saying proudly, 'A man in this house has given his life for his country'. Window after window. Newport was the same, with over two thousand men killed, many more injured. So many grieving families. Things would never be the same.

World War One was the first modern war that would require both men and women to be active participants. The contribution of all would be essential. Women, young and old, rich and poor, volunteered at home and abroad.

Newport has produced many wonderful, outstanding women. Some, like Margaret Mackworth, who became Lady Rhondda, and the very brave nurse Annie Brewer, have had their lives and achievements well documented. Others remain in the shadows. While the lives of the more well-known are justly celebrated, it is others I wish to bring into the light. More specifically, forgotten women who left their mark on Newport during World War One.

The war was desperately traumatic and the citizens of Newport were deeply involved through the four devastating years. It's impossible to know how many Newport women volunteered to help the war effort between 1914 and 1918. There were those who served in Newport, in the munitions factories and hospitals, for instance, and those who volunteered to go where they were sent, as nurses and later, in the Services. Most came home again, some died at home in the immediate aftermath of the war, others never came home.

© *Newport Reference Library*

In Newport Reference Library is a beautiful book, the Roll of Honour, listing the men and women who gave their lives in the Great War.

Despite the best efforts of its compilers in 1923, the list is incomplete as only four women are listed and there were certainly six, possibly seven, Newport women who died.

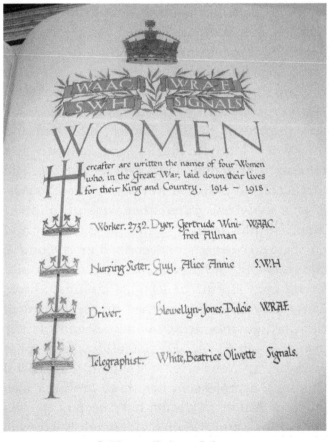

© *Newport Reference Library*

CHAPTER 1

Caroline Maud Edwards

The first Newport woman to die in service was Caroline Maud Edwards. Her connection with Newport is the most tenuous of the seven, although both her parents were from Newport families. Her mother, Erena Ellen Jones, was born and lived at 6, Capel Street in Newport until her marriage in Bassaleg in 1878. Erena's husband, Evan Prosser Edwards, a mariner, was born in Glamorgan but while he was young, his mother, Louisa, took him and his sister Matilda and moved in with her parents, John and Jane Prosser, at 24, Hill Street, off Stow Hill in Newport. John Prosser, Evan's maternal grandfather, was an affluent man. He had been a farmer in Bassaleg and on the 1861 census is described as a *'Land & House Owner & Fund Owner'*. Both Evan and Erena grew up in comfortable circumstances, living very near each other in the centre of Newport, surrounded by family. Erena's father owned a ship *The Rescue* and was a pilot working in Newport Docks and the Bristol Channel, a profession her three brothers also entered. Family talk must have been of the sea and ships, and Erena's husband Evan was also part of this seafaring world.

After their marriage, Evan and Erena moved many times. Their first child, Matilda, was born in Liverpool but by the 1881 census, she and her parents were back in Newport, living at 22, Herbert Street, a short walk from the homes of their families. Matilda's death in infancy was registered at the St. Woolos district in Newport in 1882. Also, at the end of 1882, their first son, William Merton, was born in Newport.

The family soon moved again. In 1885, William Merton was baptised in Llanharry along with his younger sister, Gladys Erena. Gladys's birth was registered in the Llanharry district as were those of her younger siblings: Daniel Bertram, born 1886, Caroline Maud (Maud Caroline), born 1887, and Mabel, born 1888.

By the 1891 census, Caroline Maud was living in Cadoxton, near Cardiff, with her family and one servant. She was near enough to have contact with her Newport grandparents, aunts, uncles and cousins. But passenger lists show that, on 16th July of that year, Erena and the five children sailed from Liverpool on the SS *Circassian* to Quebec, a nine day crossing. This must have been a huge adventure for four year old Caroline.

In 1898, the family travelled to the US and from then on, various members of the family moved between Wales, Canada and the States. Four more daughters were born to Evan and Erena in the US. Between 1895 and 1918, Evan was going through the process of obtaining US citizenship.

Evan and Erena in the States   ©P Burraston

However, the 1901 census shows the family, including Caroline, then aged thirteen, back in Wales, living in the Rockfield district of Monmouthshire. Caroline was a pupil at Haberdashers' Monmouth School for Girls. Her sister, Mabel, married Percy Samuel Burraston in Newport in 1907. They then emigrated and the 1910 US census shows them living there with two small sons. When the family returned to the US, Caroline had decided to take a different path.

In 1911, Caroline was a nurse in The London Hospital in Whitechapel. It is very likely that, with her parents so far away, she would have spent her holidays with her Newport relatives. Both her mother's brothers, Caroline's uncles, were still living in Pill with their families. When war broke out, where would she want to be but on board a ship? So she joined the Queen Alexandra's Royal Naval Nursing Service.

Caroline Maud Edwards © *P Burraston*

The SS *Drina* was built in 1913 as a passenger liner and was the first merchant ship to be requisitioned, on 4th August 1914, by the Admiralty for use as a hospital ship. In the autumn of 1915, Caroline was on this ship which moved with others from Scapa Flow in the Orkneys to Cromarty Firth on the Scottish East Coast, to join a large number of ships at anchor there over the Christmas season.

Anchored nearby was HMS *Natal*, a cruiser, which had been used mainly for ceremonial duties prior to refitting in 1915. In the war, she was being used to patrol the North Sea.

On the afternoon of 30th December 1915, the Captain of the *Natal*, Eric Black, hosted a Christmas film show, then a novelty, inviting aboard some civilians with children and also the nurses from the *Drina*. Tragically Caroline was amongst them. During the party on board the *Natal*, ammunition exploded. The ship was torn apart and sank within five minutes. The icy cold water and the midwinter afternoon darkness hampered rescuers.

One of the transcriptions in Invergordon Naval Museum of original naval signals is:

> *5.03 pm – from Drina to Flag – three nursing sisters belonging to Drina who were on board Natal are missing...*

One hundred and seventy survivors were dragged from the freezing water. Most of the other four hundred dead were never recovered. Along with Caroline, two other nursing sisters from the *Drina* died: Eliza Millicent Elvens and Olive Kathleen Rowlett. Another of the lost was nineteen year old Seaman Ivor John Moss of 5, Bishton Street, Newport who had been serving on the *Natal* since the previous May.

This tragedy was hushed up and no stories appeared in the papers. Her family would have been informed and their distress in the States and Newport can be imagined. The *Drina*, undamaged by the nearby explosion, continued as a hospital ship until 1916 when it reverted to commercial use. Later in the war, on St David's Day, 1st March 1917, it was sunk off the coast at Milford Haven.

Probate records show Caroline left £593 10s (£63,000 in today's money) to her mother, Erena, a sizeable sum then, especially for someone twenty-eight years old. Most of her immediate family had, by then, fully settled in Port Townsend, a port on the north west coast of America. The 1920 US census shows them all living together, with the addition of Caroline's sister Mabel's three little sons.

Only her older brother, William Merton Edwards, stayed in Newport, living for a time with his uncle, Thomas Jones, Erena's brother, at 2, Milman Street, training to be a ship's pilot. He too worked in Newport Docks and the Bristol Channel, and lived, in later years, at 16, Coldra Road. His son, Caroline's nephew, also William Merton Edwards, joined the Merchant Navy and was lost at sea in World War Two.

The Chatham Memorial

Caroline is named on the Chatham Memorial.

The Plaque at Monmouth Haberdashers' School

There is also a plaque at Monmouth Haberdashers' School.

The remains of the wreck of the *Natal*, marked by a buoy, are designated as a protected place under the Protection of Military Remains Act 1986 as a war grave. In July 2000, a memorial garden, Natal Gardens, was opened in Invergordon by the famous female gardener, Charlie Dimmock.

CHAPTER 2

Lilian Kate Jones

Lilian Jones, another Newport woman, was also a nurse and her death was also caused by a tragic accident, but in a very different way.

Lily, as she was often known, was born on 11th June 1878 in Newport. Her father, William Thomas Jones, was a businessman, a building contractor. Her mother, Mary Catherine (Kate), was from Brecon. The 1881 census shows them living at 54, William Street in Pill. William was becoming increasingly prosperous, at this point employing ten men.

Lilian was the first of nine children. Gertrude Maria was born in 1879, Ethel Beatrice in 1881, William Richard in 1884, and Annie in 1886. The baptismal records of Holy Trinity, Potter Street, Pill, Newport show all five children were baptised there on 24th June 1886. By then, the family were living at 6, Rutland Place, Pill, a small street leading on to the Cardiff Road, where they continued to live for the next few years.

Another two brothers were Frederick Lindsay, born in 1888, and Charles in 1890, then finally, two more sisters, Dora Claudia in 1892 and Winifred Clare in 1895. They too were baptised in Holy Trinity.

Census records from 1891 show that, by this time, the family had a live-in servant, twenty year old Sarah Evans.

School registers from Wharf Road School show her brother William was taught there until he moved to the boys' school on 12th January 1894. Were Lilian and her other siblings educated there, too?

Winston, 9 Cardiff Road, now Tovey's Funeral Directors

Newport at that time was rapidly expanding. People were moving into the town to take advantage of the plentiful work, putting pressure on housing. New houses were also needed to ease the extreme overcrowding in poorer homes. Green fields were being built over to house them. It was a good time for builders. Her father's building business, W Jones and Son, was clearly doing well as, by the turn of the century, the family had moved to Winston, 9, Cardiff Road, while still keeping business premises in Rutland Place.

In 1899, Lilian was employed by the Post Office in Newport as a learner and in 1901, she was promoted to become a Sorting Clerk and Telegraphist. The 1901 census shows her still living at home. Post Office appointment records show she spent some time with the Post Office in London but she was back at home at the time of the 1911 census.

Prior to the twentieth century, generally speaking, middle class homes had servants, and daughters were not expected to work out-side the home. However, the invention of the typewriter and telephone meant that, increasingly, there were offices which employed women. The Post Office was a large employer of educated women, although strict rules, echoing those of society as a whole, were applied to them. For example, in larger premises like Newport, they would not have been allowed to work alongside men; instead they worked in separate areas, and arrived and left at different times. In smaller, less formal offices, of course, they would have had to work with men.

Before 1914, there were two Voluntary Aid Detachments in Newport, each consisting of twenty nurses and three officers. They were to be called upon in an emergency. When war broke out, the British Red Cross joined with the St John's Ambulance Brigade and become the Joint War Committee. Further Voluntary Aid Detachments (VADs) were formed which trained volunteers in nursing and first aid, among other things. Many of the women were from sheltered homes and perhaps surprised themselves by what they were capable of achieving. Many were women who had never left home before, who had little experience of domestic work and even less knowledge of men's bodies. They worked in hospitals and rest stations under the protection of the Red Cross. They scrubbed, cleaned, washed clothing and bedding, they emptied slops and often had to attend compulsory prayers. From 1915, VADs were paid £20 (£2,100) a year. Their board and lodging were free but they had to buy their own uniforms. The Red Cross nurse wore a long blue cotton dress with the red cross displayed on a white pinafore. A St. John's nurse's dress was grey and the brigade emblem would have been on an armband. They worked alongside regular nurses in hospitals. As the war progressed, VAD became a household word.

Soon after the start of the war, Lilian left the Post Office and joined the Voluntary Aid Detachment of the British Red Cross in Newport. Her younger sister, Dora, also volunteered for Red Cross training. In August 1915, Lily started working in the 2nd Southern General Military Hospital, in Southmead, Bristol, and at that point, she moved from Newport to Bristol.

On 6th June 1916, a warm, sunny day, she was out cycling with another nurse, her friend, Gladys Williams. They were cycling down Henbury Hill when ahead of them, they saw some pedestrians. They rang their bells and applied their brakes. Without warning, an elderly pedestrian stepped out right in front of Lily. It appears she was thrown over her handlebars and onto the road with her bicycle on top of her. Her friend rushed to her side. One woman pedestrian went for help and an ambulance was sent for. When Lily arrived, unconscious, at Bristol Infirmary, she was operated on but died later that day of a cerebral haemorrhage caused by a fractured skull. She was thirty six years old.

An inquest was held in Bristol the following day attended by her father, with the principal witness being her friend, Nurse Gladys Williams, who stated they were experienced cyclists going at an ordinary pace. Although the coroner adjourned the proceedings for a day for the authorities to trace the elderly pedestrian, he could not be found. The verdict was accidental death. In the press, there was some criticism of a group of passers-by who witnessed the accident but did not help. Lily's father wrote a letter to the *Argus* refuting this, stating the family had received many messages of sympathy.

serving their King and country, one being a lieutenant in the Lancashire Regiment, and the other in the Public Schools Battalion.

TO THE EDITOR OF THE "WEEKLY ARGUS."

Dear Sir,—Lest your heading "Aid Refused by Bristol People," in reporting this case should leave on some an unfavourable impression as to the conduct of Bristol people, will you kindly allow me to say that I shall ever retain most grateful recollections f the kindly offices and many tangible tokens of sympathy shown towards me and my family by them in so tragically sudden and sad a bereavement?—Yours truly,   W. JONES.
    Winston, Cardiff-road, Newport, June 1st, 1916.

Lilian's body was brought back to Newport and she was buried at St Woolos Cemetery.

Her father was accompanied at the service by her brother, Charles, who at that time was living in the Cotham area of Bristol. With them also were the Rector and churchwardens of Holy Trinity. The *Argus* account of the men-only funeral states that her other two brothers were away fighting, one a lieutenant in the Lancashire Regiment and the other in the Public Schools Battalion. Her brothers sent flowers, as did her mother and sisters. Flowers were also sent from various groups of staff at Southmead Military Hospital and from patients she had been nursing there, as well as staff from the Red Cross in Newport, Newport Post Office and 'her old friends of the telegraph staff'.

The family grave in St Woolos Cemetery

Her father died on 17th March 1920 and left £41,656 5s 5d (£2m) to his children, Gertrude and Charles. William had died in 1919.

Lilian's name is in the Welsh National Book of Remembrance, though not on the Newport Roll of Honour, produced in 1923. By then, the family had moved away from their Cardiff Road home and, it seems, away from Newport.

CHAPTER 3

Alice Annie Guy

Born in Pill in Newport a year after Lilian and also destined to become a nurse was Alice Annie Guy. Her father, Daniel, was also a businessman, but his business was a butcher's shop in Commercial Road.

Daniel Guy's advertisement in John's Newport Directory 1897

He came originally from Dorset and his father had been a master butcher before him. In 1877 in Newport, he had married Sarah Jones from Marshfield, whose father had been a pig dealer. Alice was their first daughter. She was baptised on 11th May 1880.

The 1881 census shows the family, consisting then of Godfrey, aged two, Alice, aged one, and a baby, Rose, aged three months, living at 141 and 140, Commercial Road. By 1891, they were living at 69, Commercial Road, presumably over the butcher's shop. At that time, they had seven children and two servants/employees. In all, Daniel and Sarah had at least ten children.

Not long after 1891, the family moved to Claremont Farm in Malpas, although Daniel kept the shop which was taken over eventually by Alice's elder brother, Godfrey, who married in 1903.

Alice's sister, Rose, was married in St Paul's Church, Commercial Street, Newport on 7th June 1910 but by this time, Alice's career as a nurse had already taken her away from home.

Alice Annie Guy © *Weekly Argus*

She trained at the Salop Infirmary in Shrewsbury and then moved to the Chester and Monsall Fever Hospital, Manchester. At the time of the 1911 census, she was a sister at Bishop Auckland Fever Hospital. From there, she went to be a Night Superintendent at the Royal Devonshire Hospital in Buxton.

Early in the war, she moved to be a sister in the Norfolk War Hospital in Norwich. This building had been a huge asylum for the mentally ill and it reverted to this use after the war. Nursing the wounded, at home and abroad, was not a job for the faint-hearted. Injuries could be devastating, there were no antibiotics and no safe blood transfusions. Nurses learned to treat shock and to care for those without hope. They sat with their dying patients and wrote down what they said. Their duty then was to write home to the family.

On 24th June 1916, Alice joined the Scottish Women's Hospital League for service in Macedonia. Her experience in a fever hospital and with the wounded would stand her in great stead. The Girton & Newnham Unit, to which she was consigned, consisted of four nursing sisters, two women orderlies and a lady motor driver. A voyage to Salonica usually took eleven days through submarine-infested seas, with the constant risk of being torpedoed. They sailed on 20th July under the French Government's protection. After changing ships in Malta, which at that time of the year must have been intensely hot, they arrived in Salonica on 5th August. Much of the work there was spent fighting malaria, a huge killer made worse by the lack of suitable clothing supplied by the allied armies.

The Scottish Women's Hospital was founded in 1914 by Dr Elsie Maud Inglis, one of the earliest qualified female medical doctors and a staunch supporter of women's suffrage. The organisation had two aims: firstly, to provide medical assistance, and secondly to promote the cause of women's rights and to help win these rights by its involvement in the war effort. Its help was refused by the British Government. Dr Inglis was told by the War Office that her help was not needed and to 'go home and sit still, woman'. Undeterred, the first unit moved into northern Serbia in January 1915 at the invitation of the French.

In March 1915, Dr Inglis visited Newport and spoke in a public meeting at the Town Hall, then sited centrally in Commercial Street. The meeting was organised by the members of the Newport branch of the National Union of Women's Suffrage Societies (NUWSS). Her purpose was to raise funds and to encourage trained nurses to volunteer. The aim was to equip and staff a Welsh unit. For that, she needed £1,500 (£160,000). She paid tribute to the British nurses already serving at the front and to the VAD nurses. She was supported by members of the Newport NUWSS, the mayor and mayoress of Newport and many other local people. At the end of the war, the units, numbering eighteen by then, were disbanded and affairs were wound up. Sadly neither Dr Inglis nor Annie Guy lived to see that; Dr Inglis died of cancer in 1917.

A former *Argus* journalist, Private AF Hunt, a soldier in the South Wales Borderers, was stationed near Salonica. He wrote an account for the paper which was printed on 29th July 1916. In it, he described the awful conditions. No rain had fallen for three months. There was 'broiling' heat and 'countless billions' of flies so it was impossible to rest. A hot, fierce wind blew dust which covered everything. Life was unbearable for himself and fellow soldiers. He longed for a sight of the 'green slopes of Twyn Barllwm'. Did Alice's family read his article and realise this was where she would arrive, just a few weeks later?

Where Alice was assigned to nurse was designed as a mobile rather than a fixed hospital and was equipped with tents and vehicles. There were about three hundred patients, a large number of whom were suffering from malaria and dysentery. Many of the staff became ill. On 12th August 1916, Alice wrote home to members of her family from Salonica. She told them she was attached to a hospital in a camp on the fringe of the battle area and had twenty-eight patients in her tent, mostly French and Serbs. She described Salonica as dirty and very hot during the daytime. There were no flowers but plenty of animals and a few little Greek children. She added, 'I am glad to say I am well.' They must have been somewhat relieved.

But within a week, she was taken ill and died of dysentery on Sunday, 20th August. Her parents, by then living at Elmswood, Field's Park Crescent, received the sad news by cable.

She was buried at the huge Lembet Road Military Cemetery which is about two kilometres north of Thessaloniki. It is known locally as 'Zeitenlik' which could be translated as 'Olive Plantation'. It is a mainly World War One Allied War Cemetery. The *Balkan News* carried an article about her funeral which took place at 6.30am on the following Tuesday. Because her unit was attached to a division of the French Army, she was buried with French military honours. The service was conducted by the Chaplain General to His Majesty's Forces in Salonica. Many staff, both British and French, attended.

The *Argus* account of this tragedy states that her brother Alfred was with the Canadian Mounted Brigade. Alfred, who had attended West Mon School, had been an apprentice butcher with his father but had joined the army in July 1902. Her brother, Mark, who had been an apprentice grocer, was a gunner in training with the Royal Fleet Auxiliary.

Her father gifted an oak memorial seat to St Paul's Church in her memory. This extract is from an old guide to St Paul's. Since then, the church has moved out of the original building and the seat, sadly, cannot be traced.

QUIS CONTRA NOS?

Memorial Oak Seat.

Near the Font is an Oak Seat the gift of Mr. & Mrs. Daniel Guy, and it has the following inscription :—

TO THE HONOUR AND GLORY OF GOD

AND

IN LOVING MEMORY OF

SISTER ALICE A. GUY, DAUGHTER OF D. & S. GUY, WHO LAID DOWN HER LIFE IN THE SERVICE OF HER COUNTRY AT SALONICA. AUGUST 20th, 1916.

For many years Mr. Guy conducted the Morning Sunday School held in the old National School Buildings.

The National School Buildings where Daniel Guy conducted the Sunday School were across the road from St Paul's. Nearby, too, was the YMCA of which Daniel was president and also involved in its fundraising activities. Throughout the war, he represented Tredegar Ward on the Board of Guardians.

Alice is named on the gravestone of her parents and sister at St Mary's Church, Malpas. She is also on the Newport Roll of Honour.

The family gravestone at St Mary's, Malpas

CHAPTER 4

Women in the services

Alice, Caroline and Lilian were nurses, a traditional occupation for women. At that time, the only military role to which women were admitted was in caring for the sick and wounded. It was accepted that nurses were needed in greater numbers in wartime and that they needed to be organised. Britain had formed the Army Nursing Service in 1881. This evolved into QAIMNS (Queen Alexandra's Imperial Military Nursing Service) and soon after, followed the QAIMNS Reserve and the Territorial Force Nursing Service. QARNNS (Queen Alexandra's Royal Naval Nursing Service) had been active for decades before Caroline enlisted. The Air Force nursing service was established in 1918. There were also the Voluntary Aid Detachments linked to the Red Cross and the St John's Ambulance Brigade. In 1914 The Scottish Women's Hospital was founded.

It wasn't until half way through the war that it was formally accepted that women could perform many other functions apart from nursing, functions normally fulfilled by men. Furthermore, that using women to do back-ground work would release more men to fight on the front line. By 1917, the army was running out of men as so many had been killed or injured. By identifying jobs which did not involve fighting, men could be released from jobs in offices, canteens, stores and as drivers and telephonists. It had been estimated that up to twelve thousand men serving in the back areas could be sent into the front line and their places taken by females.

This whole concept was controversial. Many felt that using women as nurses was fine but women should not do anything 'unfeminine'. After all, the men were fighting for women and children at home. But needs must, and women did not need to be paid as much, of course. The Women's Auxiliary Army Corps (WAAC), later called Queen Mary's Auxiliary Army Corps, was introduced by the War Office in February 1917 and established a month later as part of the British Army. It was to be made up of paid volunteers of whom eventually in excess of 50,000 were employed. The women were not to use the same ranks as men. The lowest female rank was a 'worker'.

Margaret Mackworth was appointed as the Commissioner of Women's National Service for Wales and Monmouthshire. Her aim was to recruit as many women as possible to work both on the Home Front and in the WAAC.

Whereas previously her public rhetoric was to gain support for women's votes, it became an impassioned plea for women to join the war effort. Advertisements were placed in the *Argus* urging volunteers to come forward. She organised the selection boards for the WAAC. In November 1917, the Westgate Hotel in Newport was requisitioned as a local head-quarters of the WAAC. Posters were displayed outside with urgent appeals. It was used as a hostel for dealing with recruits after their acceptance and to train three hundred clerks.

An advertisement from the South Wales Argus of 17th July 1917

In January 1918, Margaret Mackworth was promoted to head the UK-wide drive to recruit women. In April 1918, she opened a week-long war service exhibition in James Howells Department Store in Cardiff. A thousand women enrolled in the WAAC, WRAF, WRNS and Women's Land Army. In November 1918, she held a recruiting meeting in Newport.

The women were largely given routine tasks: cooking and catering, storekeeping, clerical work, telephony and administration, printing and motor vehicle maintenance. They worked at home and abroad. Only well-off women could join organisations which didn't pay, but the WAAC wanted women from all classes. The wages varied according to the position held. Cooks, waitresses and housemaids were paid £26 (£1600) a year and given free board and lodging. Those doing office jobs had to pay 14s (£44) a week for board but were paid between 25s and 34s, (£80-£110) weekly, more if she became a supervisor. Like nurses, their living conditions were often very basic and crowded. Facilities were poor. They had limited free time and were not supposed to mix with men. WAACs wore a green or khaki uniform like male soldiers, consisting of a gabardine coat

WAAC Badge

frock with a brown collar, brown shoes, stockings, gaiters, an army greatcoat and a round broad-brimmed felt hat. On the front of the hat was the WAAC badge. The skirt had to be no more than twelve inches from the ground.

CHAPTER 5

Gertrude Winifred Allam Dyer

One Newport volunteer was Gertrude Dyer. Gertrude and her twin sister, Ethel, were born on 9th January 1880. Ethel was quickly baptised that day and died shortly afterwards. Gertrude's baptism took place at St John the Evangelist in Maindee on 5th February. The 1881 census shows her living in Glebe Street, Maindee, with her father, Frederick Charles Dyer, an engine fitter, and her mother, Julia Sarah, a dressmaker. Her parents had been married in 1879 and the twins were the first of at least seven children. Mabel Gwenllian was born in 1881. She was baptised in St John's that year and in 1906, married Thomas Isaac there, leaving Newport to live in Lincolnshire. Gertrude's next sister, Isabel Frances Amy, married Thomas Hughes, a school teacher in Newport. They emigrated to Canada in 1912. Her only brother, Gordon Ivor Alfred Allman, also left home before the 1911 census. He became a tea planter in India although he frequently returned to Newport.

Gertrude did not marry but stayed at home with her family in Newport. They moved within the area many times. From Glebe Street, to Dawlish Place, then on to 24, Maindee Parade.

By 1901, they were at 52, Morden Road and by 1911, 65, Morden Road.

Gertrude's home in Morden Road

The 1911 census shows the family consisted of Frederick, then aged 54, a mechanical engineer, Sarah, then 58, Gertrude, 31, a political secretary, and her youngest two sisters: Eileen, a telephonist and Olive, a shop assistant in the Singer Sewing Machine shop. In 1915, Eileen married David Jones at St John's where she and all her siblings had been baptised. Olive married Colin Felton in June 1918. But by this time, Gertrude had left home and returned only to die.

Throughout the war, Gertrude's mother, Sarah, worked as a volunteer for the Red Cross. Records show she volunteered in August 1914 and was still working for them in 1919. She was initially based at the Red Cross Depot in Commercial Street where volunteers used borrowed sewing machines to make garments for the wounded. Many of these volunteers had worked for their living all day, then spent their evenings and weekends doing this valuable work. They also altered and repaired the men's clothes. She was later moved to the 3rd Western Hospital based at Woolaston House. Red Cross records state that she used her dressmaking skills 'mending, making, repairing and darning patients' clothes' and was described as a 'devoted voluntary worker'. She was not a wealthy woman. It was a home without servants, yet even at home, she found time for knitting for the troops.

It was said that every female in the country was patriotically knitting. The Red Cross in Newport issued wool to the munitions workers, to the girls' schools and to individuals. Finished garments were parcelled up and sent to the front.

Until Gertrude enlisted in the WAAC in August 1917, she had been, for eighteen years, the secretary of the Newport Women's Liberal

Association and secretary of the Monmouthshire Branch of the Liberal Social Council. She was probably one of the few paid, professional women secretary-organisers.

Gertrude Dyer © Weekly Argus

Despite her poor health, she had devoted herself to these organisations. She was very well known in political circles and had represented Newport at national meetings of Liberal women in London and elsewhere. Very few meetings of the Liberal Party in the Newport area took place without Gertrude, the organising secretary, who arranged events, presented reports and kept minutes.

Newport Liberal women supported women's suffrage and worked for the representation of women on those elected bodies which allowed women members, for example, Boards of Guardians and parish councils. They also aimed to protect children's interests, something Gertrude was very interested in.

In this photo Gertrude is seated, second on the left amongst the great and good of the Liberal Party in Monmouthshire ©South Wales Argus

She was a member of the most popular political party. Before the war, the Liberal Party was the party of Wales. In 1906, Wales returned thirty five Liberals out of thirty six MPs to the House of Commons. One seat was taken by the anti-war, pro-women's suffrage Labour leader, Kier Hardie. By the General Election of 1922, half of all Welsh MPs were socialists, and the Liberal Party never regained its Victorian and Edwardian pre-dominance.

Gertrude also became a flag seller. Fundraising was a feature throughout World War One, although the heyday of street collections was 1914-1915, before conscription and rationing gripped the nation. Flagday appeals supported prisoners of war, refugees, especially Belgian, the wounded, and organisations such as Red Cross and St John's. The 'flags' were usually paper, sometimes tin, silk, wool, cloth or pressed foil with a pin. To buy, wear or sell flags was a sign of patriotism. It has been estimated that the Red Cross alone raised £22 million (£1.75 billion) during the war. There is a collection of these flags in St Fagan's Museum.

After Gertrude's enlistment in the WAAC as a worker, the female equivalent of a private, she was given a period of training and then drafted to France.

Gertrude was never strong but while she was abroad, her health broke down. She was initially in hospital in France and then transferred to one in London. On Monday 21st January 1918, she was discharged on fourteen days' leave and arrived home in Newport that day in a state of collapse. Despite the efforts of her doctor, she was unconscious for most of the next few days and died on Sunday, 27th January. She was 38 years old. Her death certificate shows the cause of death to have been Bright's Disease, a kidney condition.

At her funeral, she was given full military honours. Hundreds of people lined the streets. The cortège did not follow a direct route but went from Morden Road onto Caerleon Road, then Duckpool Road to Chepstow Road and Beechwood Road to Christchurch Cemetery. Thousands assembled at the cemetery. There was an outpouring of public sympathy. Her coffin was draped with the Union Jack and on it were placed her hat and haversack. It was carried by an open car. The procession was headed by the Monmouthshire Volunteer Regiment Band and the bearers were soldiers from the Western Cavalry Barracks, followed by a contingent of the WAAC stationed in Newport. The whole event was recorded at great length in the *Weekly Argus.*

Gertrude's grave in Christchurch Cemetery

The following June, her youngest sister Olive Enid married Capt Boyd Fenton while he was home on leave from France. It was a very quiet celebration. The bride wore 'an elephant grey gabardine costume'.

Gertrude is remembered in the Newport Roll of Honour and the Welsh National Book of Remembrance.

CHAPTER 6

Frances Mary Dulcie Llewellyn-Jones

A young woman who was possibly amongst her mourners was Frances Mary Dulcie Llewellyn-Jones. She would almost certainly have known the Dyer family as her father, the Reverend David Ernest Llewellyn-Jones, was vicar of St John the Evangelist, Maindee, and had conducted the marriage service of Gertrude's sister, Eileen, in 1915. The family had connections with this church. They lived in the same parish and Gertrude's funeral cortège passed near the bottom of the street where Frances lived.

St John the Evangelist, Maindee

Frances was born in September 1894 in the Bridgend area. Her father was a curate at

Llandow and she was baptised in Llandow on 2nd October of that year. Her parents had married the previous year in Cardiff where her mother, Frances Eliza Sophia Morris, was from a family of solicitors in Park Place. After a further curacy at St Andrew's in Cardiff, where their second daughter, Gwenith Margaret, was born, the family moved to Newport in 1897 for the Reverend David Ernest Llewellyn-Jones to take up his appointment as vicar of St John the Evangelist, Maindee.

The Vicarage

So Frances and her sister grew up in the vicarage in St John's Road, Maindee. At only three and two years old, they would not remember any of their lives before they moved to Newport. Until she enlisted, the vicarage would be Frances' only home. Gwenith was her only sibling. They would have attended Sunday School and been involved in the life of the church.

I can find no record of where they went to school but situated in St John's Road was a girls' school. Drayton High School for Girls offered private education from kindergarten through to preparation for university. Maybe this was considered convenient and suitable?

The 1911 census shows the four of them at the vicarage with two live-in servants - a cook and a parlour maid. Frances was sixteen and Gwenith fifteen. Aside from his clerical duties, her father played golf and in 1907, had been captain of Newport Golf Club, then situated at Great Oak, Rogerstone. His hobby was astronomy. He attended meetings to support the NSPCC and was concerned about child welfare. Sadly, it is not known whether Frances or Gwenith had similar interests.

Rev David Ernest Llewellyn-Jones
© John's Who's Who in Newport Directory 1920

The *Weekly Argus* of 9th October 1912 states he chaired a meeting of the suffragists in the Temperance Hall in Newport where the main speaker was Frederick Pethick Lawrence, a man not long out of prison where he had been placed because of involvement with the law-breaking activities of the Women's Social and Political Union. He was later dismissed from this organisation because he did not agree with its methods. Sybil Haig Thomas was on the platform, too. She was president of the Welsh Union of Women's Liberal Associations, which was strongly feminist and pro-female suffrage. She was also a member of the WSPU. This suggests Frances's father was open-minded regarding the equal role of women in society - a good thing for the five women living in the vicarage with him! It also suggests another link with Gertrude Dyer who, as a Liberal woman, probably held similar views and could even have been at this meeting, as indeed could Frances.

Less than a fortnight before the start of the war, Maindee Parish Church held a Garden Fête to raise money for a new organ. Rev Llewellyn-Jones, in a telephone conversation, had persuaded Miss Marjorie Lysaght, aged 23, to open the fete. She was accompanied by her mother and her father, Mr William Lysaght, owner of the Orb Steelworks which at the time employed 3,000 people. There was fun and laughter. All the female members of the Llewellyn-Jones family were there helping on stalls. Frances and Gwenith helped to serve teas. No doubt, daughters of the wealthy and of clergymen were expected to take on such roles. But the war changed everything.

In what a different tone is the account of the dedication of the new organ in October. The music was suitable for wartime and interspersed with silent time for private prayers and reflections. Already the Orb Works had started its roll of honour and it was not long before Rev Llewellyn-Jones was conducting funerals for the war dead of the parish. A huge procession and memorial service at St John's was held in May 1915 for those of the parish and others of the 1st Battalion of the Monmouthshire Regiment who had already died. Happy pre-war days were over.

By the summer of 1916, it became clear that the war effort needed far more VAD nurses. Appeals for volunteers appeared nationally in the press. Parents were urged to allow their daughters to volunteer. Existing nurses in auxiliary hospitals were asked to work full time so that other nurses could be released to serve in the military hospitals. Like Lilian Jones the previous year and many other women, Marjorie Lysaght and her younger sister, Alison, volunteered as Red Cross nurses. So, too, did Gwenith Llewellyn-Jones, Frances's sister.

Llanwern Park House, a mansion set on a hill overlooking Newport, home of Sybil and David Thomas, had been used by their daughter, Margaret Mackworth, for her suffragette rallies and fundraising events, but at the beginning of the war the Thomases turned part of it into an auxiliary hospital. Early in 1917, Gwenith was working at Llanwern Park Red Cross Hospital as a VAD nurse. As there was only one trained nurse, the matron, Salla Poole, in Llanwern at this time, the VADs must have performed highly skilled work as well as the usual routine tasks. Gwenith moved from Llanwern to the 1st London Hospital, Camberwell. This was a military hospital established in a former college, St Gabriel's, where, in her famous novel *Testament of Youth*, Vera Brittain, then a VAD, described nursing her brother Edward. Later in the war, Gwenith worked in Bishop's Court Auxiliary Hospital in Alresford, Hampshire. No doubt her letters home to the vicarage in Maindee contained sad accounts of the wounded men she was caring for.

In April 1918, one of the church's wealthy parishioners, who had lost two sons at the front, donated a huge sum to the church as well as a carved oak reredos and a carved oak communion table. Many parishioners of all classes would have been bereaved and the thoughts of many were turning to how such sacrifices could be remembered. Rev Llewellyn-Jones was a founder member of the Newport Roll of Honour committee, which had its first meeting in Maindee School on 20th July 1918.

What Frances did at the start of the war is unclear. At her funeral, there were flowers from 'the doctor, Matron and staff' of Beechwood Hospital, a sanatorium for soldiers and munitions workers with tuberculosis, of which her father was chaplain. Perhaps Frances also volunteered there. What is clear is that she enlisted on 23rd August 1918 in the Women's Royal Air Force (WRAF), an organisation only formed on 1st April that year. The first Women's Royal Air Force was an auxiliary organisation of the Royal Air Force. The original intent of the WRAF was to provide female mechanics in order to free up men. However, it saw huge enrolment, with women volunteering for positions as drivers and mechanics and filling other wartime needs. This first WRAF was disbanded in 1920 but Frances was not to live to see that.

On 27th September, she was sent to Saltley College, Birmingham, a former Church of

England teacher training college used during the war by the military. From there, she was sent on 19th October to No 7 Stores Depot, Mexborough, Yorkshire as a motor driver.

By this time, the great influenza pandemic was sweeping through the world. There were numerous cases in Newport. The Royal Gwent Hospital stated it could take no more wounded men as it was full with civilians. In July 1918, the *Argus* declared flu was 'ravaging' the country. There were further reports in October. It seemed to have been particularly dangerous for young adults as these died in disproportionate numbers. All the poor, cramped living conditions experienced by service personnel, and some civilians, contributed to its spread, as did all the travel associated with conflict. It has been estimated that the pandemic killed more people than the war.

As the war was ending, Frances contracted influenza and was taken into Montagu Auxiliary Hospital, Mexborough. Her father rushed to her side and was with her when she died on 13th November, two days after the armistice. She was twenty four years old. Her body was brought back to Newport.

Her funeral was held on Monday, 18th November at 12 noon at St John's. Her father, of course, was there, dressed in khaki as

chaplain of the First Battalion Monmouthshire
Regiment, but he did not conduct the service.
That was done by the vicar of St Woolos. As
can be imagined, the funeral was well
supported by the local clergy. The ladies of the
church covered the altar with flowers and the
full choir sang. Her coffin was draped with the
Union Jack and on it was placed the family
tribute: a cross of pink chrysanthemums.
After the service, they processed to Christchurch Cemetery. Flowers had been sent by
her family and friends, colleagues at
Mexborough, various local Sunday Schools
and 'the working party of St John's Red
Cross', amongst others.

The family grave in Christchurch Cemetery

On the Imperial War Graves Commission report of 1925, details of Frances' headstone are listed on the same page as Gertrude Dyer's. Frances's death is recorded on the Newport Roll of Honour.

The family grave in Christchurch Cemetery

Gwenith survived the war but her mother died less than two years after Frances, leaving her living at home with just her father who carried on with his duties in the church and in the wider community. She married in 1929 and moved to Cardiff just before the death of her father in 1930. He left £5,613.00 (£327,000) to Gwenith and her husband, John Morris.

CHAPTER 7

Beatrice Olivette White

Less than fifteen minutes' walk from Maindee Vicarage, and a few hundred yards from Gertrude Dyer's home, was the home of another young lady who answered the appeal for female volunteers. She would not, however, have witnessed Gertrude's funeral procession, even though it passed her front door; she had enlisted in the WAAC a few months earlier.

Beatrice Olivette White was born in the summer of 1886. She seems to have used the name Beatrice most of the time, certainly in formal situations, but was known familiarly as Olive. Her father, William Isaac White, a grocer's assistant from Cornwall, had married Eliza Edwards from Caerleon in 1880. They settled down in 63, Blewitt Street, Baneswell in Newport. Their first daughter, Lilian Agnes, was born in 1880. There were no other surviving children until the birth of Beatrice. After that, they had three sons: Reginald William in 1890, Stanley Egerton in 1895 and Trevor Henderson in 1898.

On the 1891 census, the family were living just off the Caerleon Road at 11, Constance Street and William described himself as a grocer. By the 1901 census, he was a self-employed grocer but, as a sign of the changing times, he then moved his family to 149, Caerleon Road - the Post Office. William was then a newsagent and sub-postmaster.

The Post Office in 2017 - Beatrice's family home

Post Office Appointment Books show that others in the family also made their careers in the Post Office. Lilian became a telegraph clerk, initially in Newport, but later records show she was working for the Post Office in Bexhill-on-Sea. Two of her brothers were also employed by the Post Office.

Beatrice joined the Post Office in Newport as a learner in 1903 when she was seventeen years old and, by the summer of 1906, she was a telephone operator. In May 1907, she moved to Totnes, where she became a sorting clerk and telegraphist. This meant she was employed in a dual role to sort the mail and handle the telegraph business. From Totnes, she moved to the Pontypool office and possibly stayed at the Park Hotel there. She is recorded on the 1911 census as living at home.

While Beatrice was working in Pontypool, the *Times* newspaper of 5th March 1913 reported that, as part of the suffragette action in South Wales, women cut the telephone wires between Newport and Pontypool, causing much disruption. It would be really interesting to know how Beatrice viewed this. By 1914, at the outbreak of war, she was again working in Newport at the General Post Office. Would she have known Lilian Jones? Both were working in the same department at the same time. She cannot fail to have heard about Lilian's death in 1916. Also working there at that time as a telephonist, was Eileen Dyer, Gertrude's sister. She lived just around the corner from Beatrice near the bottom of Morden Road.

Trevor White, aged seventeen, enlisted in 1914 in the Monmouthshire Regiment and served with them until March 1917 when he was diagnosed with an inflammation of connective tissue of his right hand. He was put on an ambulance train home. Both Reginald and Stanley had by that time also enlisted.

On 2nd November 1917, Beatrice enlisted in the WAAC and was soon sent to France, as a signaller-telegraphist. With her experience, she was a real asset. She would probably have worn a two-tone white and blue arm-band, indicating a person engaged on signals work.

In Newport, the recruiting of women continued. The *Weekly Argus* of 27th April 1918 showed a large photograph of a group of jolly local WAACs. It carried advertisements in June and July, promising free training, good wages and comfortable accommodation. This was followed in August by a very upbeat article sent to the *Argus* by an anonymous, local woman, describing her experiences on joining the WAAC. She wrote that women went before medical and selection boards and, if fit, were sent a one-way rail ticket to a WAAC depot in Britain, where training began. They were vaccinated and drilled into army life. All was in preparation for serving abroad. She made it sound like a thrilling adventure and wrote they couldn't wait to be posted overseas.

Beatrice was stationed at Abbeville, on the Somme, in northern France, the headquarters of the Commonwealth lines of communication, and she remained there during the 1917/18 winter. She was there during the dark days of the German offensive in March. The WAACs were told to leave but would not desert their posts, even though there were nightly raids. Later, she was transferred to Calais. In May 1918, she was granted some leave and came home. While she was at home, she became ill. Her commandant in Abbeville wrote to her:

> *I am sorry that you do not get strong. I shall never forget you during the winter in AB. I realised how you suffered in those cold and rough surroundings, and appreciated your courage more than you knew perhaps. I have been thanking the girls for all their personal loyalty to me, which helped me no end; and I certainly want to include you in my thanks - your work was always so absolutely reliable. It meant so much to me to number you amongst those on whom I could really lean with confidence. Thank you very much for all your help, and the example of your courage and endurance during those hard times.*

Her health must have remained poor as she was discharged medically unfit on 8th August 1918 and returned to her post office job until November, dying on 29th November. On her death certificate, the cause of death is noted as influenza pneumonia. The doctor has also written that her temperature had reached 108.8F, over ten degrees above normal and way above danger level.

In her obituary in the *Weekly Argus,* headed 'Patriotic Girl', the journalist states that her health was 'undoubtedly undermined in her country's service'.

Her funeral was held on Thursday, 5th December. There was a service in the family home before the male mourners proceeded to Christchurch Cemetery for the internment service, both led by Rev Verrant Wills, a Wesleyan Methodist minister. Her brother Trevor was there but the *Argus* account does not mention Reginald nor Stanley. Had they still not returned from their army postings? All three brothers survived the war.

Beatrice's grave in Christchurch Cemetery

There is a memorial plaque in St Julian's Methodist Church on Caerleon Road with her name inscribed on it and *'Post Sec RE'*. The members of the church to whom I spoke when I photographed the plaque, referred to her as *Olive* and this name has been used as a decorative addition on her gravestone.

The plaque in St Julian's Methodist Church

The church magazine of January 1919 said:

> *The sympathy of members of the Church will be extended to Mr White, leader of the Wednesday evening Adult Class, in the loss he has sustained through the death of his daughter, which occurred as a result*

of illness arising from the prevailing epidemic.

Beatrice is named in the Newport Roll of Honour.

CHAPTER 8

Violet Phillips

The last of the female Newport casualties of the war, Violet Phillips, was also the youngest.

Violet's father, Edgar Phillips, was from a long-established Newport family. His father had been a coal merchant from Bassaleg. He was comfortably off and a magistrate. Edgar grew up in Newport and in all, he had at least twelve siblings. The 1881 census shows him, aged nineteen, living with his family at 176, Commercial Road and his occupation is described as a 'clerk to merchant'. Ten years later, still living at home, he described himself as a 'bookkeeper and accountant'. He was a man who worked to better himself.

On 1st February 1892, he married Charlotte Maria Cox, aged nineteen, in St Paul's Church, Newport, where he had been baptised thirty years earlier. She had been born in Bedminster in Bristol but her family had moved to Newport when she was a child. Her father, Joseph, had been a gardener in the grounds of Bellevue House, now incorporated into Bellevue Park. At the time of her marriage, Charlotte and her family were living at Trinity Place, St Woolos.

Edgar and Charlotte's first child, Dorothy, was born in 1896 and then on 29th August 1898, Violet arrived. At the time of her baptism in St Paul's, the four of them were living at Llanbedr House, 47, Devon Place, a large red brick terraced property near the railway station. Edgar's occupation entered on her baptismal certificate is 'cashier'.

By the 1901 census, Edgar was an 'Engineers Clerk'. They had moved to 79, Caerau Road, a large property at the very bottom of the hill where Caerau Road joins Clytha Park Road. By then, Violet had another sister, Gladys. Also living with them was a cousin, Dorothy Yeomans, aged thirteen, Edgar's sister's daughter. Dorothy was soon to leave Newport to train as a midwife but returned years later to live with her mother and sister in Preston Avenue. Violet's paternal grandparents were living in 28, Ombersley Road so she grew up surrounded not only by the friends and relatives living with them, but also a very large extended family living within walking distance.

On 9th January 1905, Dorothy and Violet were admitted to Clytha School on Bryngwyn Road which had opened a few years earlier, in 1901, for three hundred and twenty pupils. Violet was then six years old. The school records show that, prior to this date, the girls had been educated privately. At home, there was another new sister, Doris. In all, Violet had four sisters and one brother, Clarence, born last, on 14th December 1909.

At the time of the 1911 census, Edgar is a 'clerk incorporated accountant' and the family, Edgar, Charlotte, Dorothy, Violet, Gladys, Doris, Violet's youngest sister Charlotte Evelyn, and Clarence, were living at Arundel Villa, 32, Barrack Hill.

Violet's family home on Barrack Hill

With them there were also Joseph Cox, Violet's maternal grandfather, then sixty seven years old, and a cousin, Charlotte Hurley, aged twenty four. The rest of the Hurley family were living at 9, Clytha Crescent. Also with them were three, very young cousins who were some of the children of Isabella Bland, Violet's aunt, who, with her husband, ran a bakery and confectioners business in Newport: Bland's Restaurant. The Bland family ran The Silver Grill on the corner of High Street and Station Approach and also The Mikado in High Street. Violet would have been surrounded by family: a grandfather, siblings and cousins as well as her parents. It was a house full of people.

In April 1917, when Violet was eighteen years old, she successfully passed an examination in the Great Western Railway Ambulance Class. She and some of her classmates were formally presented with badges at an evening ceremony in High Street, (now Central) Station in June. Throughout the war, the GWR worked with St John's Ambulance Brigade to provide and service the ambulance trains. These specially-adapted trains could be up to a third of a mile long, and included wards, pharmacies, emergency operating rooms, kitchens and staff accommodation. The ambulance trains calling in Newport often continued to Cardiff and Neath.

Barrack Hill is very steep but it is not a particularly long road. However, it had its share of casualties. In October 1914, the Phillips's next door neighbours at Number 30 received the news that their son, Francis, had been killed. The following May, their neighbours at Number 36 lost their son, Charles. People must have lived in suspense. Every ring of the doorbell could be a telegram. In all, seven men from Barrack Hill died, the final one, in October 1918, being eighteen year old John from across the road in Number 33. They must have thought their community had suffered more than enough, but there was one more death to come.

The closest sibling to Violet in age was Dorothy, who had been a Red Cross nurse since before the war. Perhaps it was Dorothy's marriage on 29th October 1917 to William Henry Deakin that prompted Violet to enlist in the WAAC (QMAAC). Like Gertrude Dyer and Beatrice White, she is described on her forces records as a worker. She was posted to Chadderton Camp near Oldham, a training centre for recruits on an old golf course taken over by the military, where she was employed as a clerk.

The date she returned home, and the reason, is not recorded, but it was at home at 32, Barrack Hill that she died on 8th March 1919, while still a member of QMAAC. She was twenty years old and the final, tragic casualty of the Great War on Barrack Hill. Her death certificate gives the causes of death as acute pneumonia/tuberculosis and cardiac failure. She was buried at St Woolos Cemetery. The Imperial War Graves Commission documentation indicates that on her headstone was to be a cross inscribed with a text.

Violet's gravestone in St Woolos Cemetery

There was the briefest of notices of her death in the *Argus* and sadly I could find no record of her funeral as the relevant editions of the *Weekly Argus* have been lost.

Her father, Edgar, died in 1929 by which time the family were living at 7 Cardiff Road. He left £81 6s 8d (£4,700) to his widow, Charlotte, and only son, Clarence.

CHAPTER 9

Most came home safely

Thankfully, these seven were the only Newport female fatalities. We may never know exactly what motivated them to serve their country in the way they did. Perhaps it was sheer human compassion; perhaps a heightened sense of patriotism meant they were affected by the appeals for volunteers; perhaps they had loved ones at the front; perhaps they wanted to show they were the equal of men; perhaps they longed for adventure and saw enlistment as a way to leave home. Whatever their reasons, they showed great bravery. It is a further tragedy that some of their graves are so sadly neglected.

At the outbreak of war, women became increasingly involved in the lives of strangers and began to break out of what must have seemed permanently fixed lifestyles. Many women had been agitating for change, but for the most part women's roles were what they had always been. The opportunities offered by war gave women the chance to get out of their homes and onto a wider stage. Single women could enlist in the services like Gertrude Dyer, Beatrice White, Frances Llewellyn-Jones and Violet Phillips. And there were women like

Lilian Jones, Dorothy Phillips, the Lysaght sisters and Gwenith Llewellyn-Jones who volunteered as Red Cross nurses, locally and further afield.

Many of the Newport women, who enlisted in the services or volunteered as nurses, served abroad and returned home safely. For example, Winifred May Price who grew up in Newport where her father, Thomas, was a Congregational minister. She was about seventeen years old when she volunteered with the Scottish Women's Hospital in July 1915. She nursed in Serbia with Elsie Inglis and was awarded the Serbian Cross of Mercy.

There was also Bertha Davies from Garth Hill, Fairoak Terrace, Bassaleg, who was a VAD nurse. Her duties took her, like Lilian Jones, to the Southern General Hospital in Bristol but after that, she volunteered to go to the military hospital in Cairo. The ship she was on was torpedoed in the eastern Mediterranean. Many lives were lost but she survived and continued her journey overland from Alexandria to Cairo. She wrote a letter home describing her adventures. Bertha stayed in Cairo after the war and was married there in January 1919 to Rev G A Elliot, the Wesleyan chaplain to the forces in the Far East.

May Stratford, who was born in Newport in the autumn of 1898, enlisted in February

1918, transferring later to the WRAF. She lived in Farmwood Cottages, 1, Bolts Row, Chepstow Road. May returned to Newport in September 1919 and lived until she was eighty four.

These women were all single, but married women, too, made their mark, although previously they would have been obliged to give up work on marriage. Some were trained nurses like Florence Horden.

Florence had been born in 1874 in Shropshire and had qualified as a nurse. In 1907, she moved to Newport when she married Frederick Horden, the manager of Barclays Bank in High Street. They lived at 21, Bassaleg Road.

Frances Horden
© *John's Who's Who in Newport Directory 1920*

Their only son was born in 1909. At the start of the war, she volunteered to resume her nursing and became the superintendent of the Red Cross Hospital at Brynglas House. It accommodated over forty beds for nursing wounded and convalescing soldiers. Florence was also in charge of some of the nurses' training given by the Red Cross. A number of the nurses she trained went to France to work in the hospitals nearer the front. In addition to her nursing, Florence was a member of the Newport Infantile Health Committee. She was awarded the MBE by the King in Buckingham Palace on 6th March 1918.

Newport women lived interesting lives at an interesting time. They rose to the challenge of those times and were deeply involved in the life of Newport with its array of organisations, groups and establishments.

CHAPTER 10

Munitionettes

At the outset of war, Britain was ill-equipped in terms of field artillery and shells so the government took over the production of munitions. In May 1915, the government created the Ministry of Munitions with David Lloyd George as minister. In the summer of 1915, Uskside Engineering Company premises, previously used for producing equipment for coal mines, was acquired by the government as a munitions factory. It was already running night and day producing shells, and the output was to be rapidly expanded. By July 1915, it employed two hundred and thirty women round the clock in the manufacture of shells and ships' forgings.

In August 1915, all women as well as men in Britain, between sixteen and sixty five years old, were required to register their names, ages and occupations. This was a public acknowledgement that the female contribution to the war effort was necessary.

Some women were formally trained in the engineering workshop of Newport Technical Institute (which later became the Art College). They attended afternoon classes along with men for about three weeks. Other training was given to women in evening classes at other engineering premises in the town. The *Weekly Argus* article of 15th October 1915 describing this, announced, rather breathlessly, 'The day of woman has arrived'.

That same month, the Newport National Shell Factory in Maesglas was established and its first output was in June 1916. It employed women on three eight-hour shifts. Originally, it was based in engine sheds belonging to the Great Western Railway Company and a factory owned by CH Bailey: the Tyne Engineering Works.

Early in 1917, the National Cartridge and Box Repair Factory started operations employing 3,000 to 4,000 people, 85% of whom were female.

The female workers, manufacturing the equipment of war, were known as 'munitionettes' and although the work was unpleasant and unhealthy, it had a certain status. They knew the work was of national importance. They would have worn the triangular On War Service badge.

Accidents happened but were hushed up. There was no emphasis on health and safety in those days. Protective clothing was unheard of. The munitionettes sometimes wore trousers but these, for modesty, had to be covered by a tunic.

Minnie Susan Sanders standing 2nd from the left - note the shells in this photo © *Melodie Neale*

They worked excessively long hours. In April 1916, the local MP, Lewis Haslam, queried in Parliament the number of hours worked by the munitions workers and also the lack of facilities available for them. He was told improvements were being considered. Again in June, he spoke against 'an undue amount of overtime' which was bad for the health of the employees and also caused a drop in productivity. This was addressed to the Minister for Munitions, David Lloyd George.

But, if the conditions were poor, the wages were good, much better than the women would have been used to before the war at £2-£3 (£200-£280) per week. This meant they could afford luxuries and nights out. As a comparison, women working in shops in Newport were generally paid considerably less than £1 (£95) for a 59-hour week. Many were paid less than ten shillings (£47).

The women who were employed in the factories were not only paid more but were also able to take advantage of the recreational opportunities. Women played football. Pictures from that time show lady footballers wearing loose shorts and roomy tops. Records exist of 'friendly' games against Swansea women. There is also a record of a rugby match between the women working in the National Cartridge and Box Factory in Newport against a Cardiff women's team. The proceeds went to the Royal Gwent Hospital which was then a charitable institution relying on subscriptions, donations and fundraising events such as these. There were other friendly matches often raising sizeable sums for charities and Newport was particularly successful with its women's hockey team. There was a tennis club, and being Wales, there was a choir.

Professional photographs of the munitions workers were taken from time to time but the individual women were not usually identified by name. Descendants however have identified some: Minnie Susan Sanders, Evelyn Ellis, Ethel and Susie Davis.

Susie and Ethel were sisters. Their parents had died so they lived, with another sister, Elsie, in the home of their 85-year-old maternal grandfather, John Nicholls, in 62, Morden Road. Did they know Gertrude Dyer and her sisters at number 65? Susie had been a shop assistant before she started working in munitions. Ethel later married Tom Wilkinson and moved to Cardiff.

Ethel Eleanor Davies is on the left of the front row
© Michael Wilkinson

Evelyn Ellis was born in June 1895 and lived in 56, Alma Street in Newport. Her father, William, was a carpenter and joiner. She was the eldest child in her family and she attended both Tredegar Wharf and Bolt Street Schools. Evelyn married Arthur 'Reg' Young at the beginning of 1918. Her grandson runs the excellent Newport Past website.

Minnie Susan Sanders had been born in Devon in 1892. Her mother had died when she

was a child and her Aunt Susan, a cook, lived
with the family. Her father remarried in 1909

Seated: Evelyn Hiley Ellis, nursing a shell © *Nigel Young*

and about this time, Minnie left home.
Perhaps it was from her aunt that Minnie
acquired her skills, for she started work as a
cook at the home of a Newport solicitor,
Maurice Allen, at 13, Oakfield Road. This
position had been found for her by a relative,
possibly the father of Lilian Christine

Mogridge, another young servant in 13 Oakfield Road. Lilian's father came originally

Minnie Susan Sanders   © Melodie Neal

from Devon but had settled with his family at 2, Crown Street, Maindee. Minnie was friendly with this family. Lilian gave Minnie her autograph book which has entries for the years up to 1916 when they worked together for Maurice Allen. This book is now treasured by her granddaughter in Australia.

In 1916, Minnie, like so many other women, left domestic service and started work in the newly opened Newport National Shell Factory. After the war, she returned to Devon and was married in 1921.

CHAPTER 11

Peace Movements

Little is known about the Newport women who opposed the war. They were certainly in a minority and greatly criticised. Maybe some of the women described in this book were in two minds about the war. In the autograph book of Minnie Sanders, the servant who became a munitions worker, there is an entry which reflects a certain cynicism regarding the official, patriotic line. It was written on the 27th April 1916 by a friend of Minnie's, Mabel Willis.

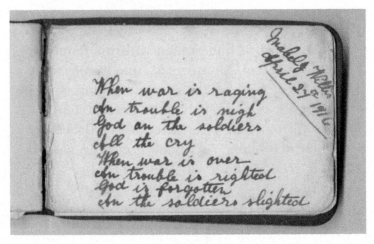

© Melodie Neal

When war is raging
An(d) trouble is nigh
God an(d) the soldiers
All the cry
When war is over
An(d) trouble is righted
God is forgotten
An(d) the soldiers slighted.

The sentiments in this are pretty clear, but finding out what other women actually thought and felt is difficult, possibly because many women, especially those on the higher rungs of the social ladder, would have kept such unpopular views to themselves. Another difficulty for researchers is that organised anti-war groups often had to hold their meetings in secret and newspapers were too patriotic to report, other than negatively, on organisations and individuals who criticised the war.

Opposition to the war politically came from the Independent Labour Party, a group within the main Labour Party. Opposition also came from some women's rights and suffrage groups. Nationally, at the outbreak of war, both Emmeline Pankhurst of the WSPU and Millicent Fawcett, leader of the NUWSS, urged their members to cease pro-suffrage activities and support the war effort. Not all their members agreed. Some actively worked to bring a peaceful end to the war. Sylvia Pankhurst, of the WSPU, remained steadfastly opposed to the hostilities. Another woman, Catherine Marshall, resigned from the NUWSS and helped to organise the Women's Peace Conference in The Hague in the Spring of 1915. Out of this grew The Women's League for Peace and Freedom.

Catherine Marshall was also involved in the No-Conscription Fellowship. Many women were active in this organisation which offered moral and physical support to families and also campaigned against the harsh treatment and imprisonment of conscientious objectors (COs). Conscription was introduced at the beginning of 1916 and there were many and varied reasons for men refusing to join the army when their conscription orders arrived: some reasons were religious, some political and some ethical. They were hunted down if they went into hiding and faced severe punishments. Their families faced outright hostility from friends and neighbours.

There was an active branch of the No-Conscription Fellowship in Newport. One of its members was Archie B Moon of 5, Brynhyfryd Avenue, who was dismissed by Newport Education Committee from his post as a teacher for his pacifist views. He had been a

member of the Board of Guardians, representing Tredegar Ward along with Daniel Guy.
He faced courts martial twice, once in October
1916 at Kinmel Park, Abegele and once in
September 1917 at Oswestry.

Another member was Albert E Rundall, a
brewer's labourer, who lived at 151,
Shaftesbury Street with his parents, Tom and
Emma, and his younger sister, Rose. His two
elder brothers had enlisted in 1915. Alfred
was probably the subject of much hatred by
many in the local community where he would
have been branded traitor and coward. He was
sentenced to two years' hard labour and this
probably caused his premature death in 1918.

Florence Jones © Marie Skinner

Alfred and Esther Jones, living at 186, Shaftsbury Street, would have been sympathetic. Their daughter, Florence Elizabeth, was an active member of the No-Conscription Fellowship.

She was eighteen years old when conscription was imposed. Her fiancée, Harry Myles Riding of 12, Arundel Road, had refused to enlist and went into hiding, supported by his family and Florence's.

Florence worked in an office in Newport. She kept a little notebook during this period in which she recorded details of the con-scientious objectors in Newport, including Archie Moon and Alfred Rundall. She and other members of the No-Conscription Fellowship, male and female, organised regular, secret meetings in Newport where news of local conscientious objectors, already imprisoned, was read out and messages of support sent. Members monitored the prisoners' wellbeing as closely as they could. There was clearly a network of supporters throughout South Wales and, it seems, there were at least forty people in the Newport support group. They visited the prisons, wrote letters and sent parcels.

When Florence started to write in her little notebook on 30th April 1916, six men, in-cluding Albert Rundall, from the Newport NCF had been arrested that day and held in the cells in Dock Street Police Station. Their supporters, including many women, were trying unsuccessfully to get them bailed. After further imprisonment in Cardiff, the men were transferred to Rhyl. At that stage Harry Riding, her fiancé, was still free.

© Marie Skinner

May 12th Friday

Heard from the boys at Rhyl. Going on still cheerful. Had refused to put on khaki. Taken before the Colonel to state their position to be court martialled. Promised to give them notice when it would happen. Friday Harry heard the police would be coming for him over the W/E. Also W Pope seeing he did not expect the military to accept his certificate from the Doctor. Another letter from Com Reynolds on his way to Rhyl with Councilor Jenkins.

Saturday May 13

More letters from Rhyl. All going on quite well. Com Rundall said they have been in a few scrapes but <u>their chins were still unscraped.</u> They had been out for exercise. He said he had caught sight of Com Reynolds but that was all...

Sunday May 14

Harry still quite safe. Again able to go to S. School to wish them another Good Bye. Sunday night, letters read out from those at Rhyl. Also one from Com Reynolds. We heard that a neighbours son from Mt Ash was with our boys from Npt. He had had a very rough time.

The civil and military police scoured Newport and Harry was taken into custody on 26th May. Florence, her mother, his family and friends shadowed him round Newport until he was taken onto the train for Cardiff at about 6 pm. About thirty supporters were on the platform at Newport Station to see him off.

Sunday June 11

Nearly too tired to get up Letter from Harry. They would not give it to me until I went down. Soon up then. Not much news. Lovely morning

Went to school after dinner which was very good. being Whit Sunday. All children very excited when they heard to the tea they were to have. Several Adults present. After school went home to tea, Alice with me. Tea over & we had a little music & then set off for meeting together. Clifford Allen the speaker.

© *Marie Skinner*

Clifford Allen was the Newport-born national chair of the No-Conscription Fellowship. He was imprisoned three times as a conscientious objector.

He saw me when I went in & told me he had been to Cardiff in the afternoon & went to Barracks but was unable to see My Boy. Managed to see Morgan Jones.

Very fine meeting. Room absolutely packed.

Com Griffiths read a letter from Harry that he had received.

C Allen afterwards shouted 3 Cheers for those in Custody & the room was in a roar of cheers loud enough to be heard by those away. - Well, meeting over I had a talk with C Allen. Oh! Mrs Salter was also present & gave a short address. I met Miss M Hemprick. Rather exciting time with her.

Monday June 12

Day of Harry's Court Martial. His mother and Mamma going down & I had to go to work which was very much against ...

Florence managed to get the afternoon off work and went to Cardiff's Maindy Barracks to join Harry's family and supporters. He was sentenced to hard labour in Dartmoor Prison. She ended her account on Tuesday 13th June.

After the war ended, Harry Riding was released. He and Florence were married in 1920 and settled down at 232, Christchurch Road, which has since been demolished. They had one child, a son, Wilfred Jones Riding, who, in his turn, was also a conscientious objector in the Second World War. Florence lived to be a hundred, dying in Newport in 1998.

CHAPTER 12

Newport Needed Women

Even before conscription started, so many men had volunteered that there were all sorts of openings for women. It was with hesitancy that Newport Post Office used women to sort the mail in the run up to Christmas 1914. As an 'experiment', it chose thirty sixteen to twenty-two year old women for three weeks and seemed surprised at how well they could sort the mail. Also due to the men shortage, it moved young women from the telegraph and telephone departments to work on the public counters. Already women were emerging.

Of course, working class women were more accustomed to work outside the home. The work they did was usually unskilled and this therefore was the justification for paying them less. As well as domestic service, they worked in factories, laundries and mills. Married working women with no servants had to fit their jobs around their demanding duties at home - and there were no labour-saving devices in those days. Not for them the luxury of another woman to do their housework!

But with men leaving to join the army, the labour shortage in Newport meant there were better jobs to be had, and although hampered by their long skirts and tight corsets, women took their places in industry, public transport and farm work, becoming active participants in the economy. Many who had been in domestic service enjoyed the camaraderie and the better pay. Working women had freedom, could make friends and socialise. Of course, this was only for the duration as was made clear in their contracts. Also agreements with the trades unions, who fiercely protected their members' jobs while they were away, meant that, although they were doing men's work, as a matter of course they were paid less.

At the end of August 1916, the Newport Corporation Electricity and Tramways Committee decided that, as an 'experiment', women would be employed as tram conductors and after a 'fair trial', a report would be submitted. Gladys Wreford became one of the first female tram conductors. She had been born on 15th June 1899 and baptised in St Paul's Church in the same month. She attended Corporation Road School. In 1911, she was living with her family at 34, Walsall Street. Both her father and brother, John, were ships' painters in the docks. When war started John enlisted and was promoted a number of times. By 1917, he was a sergeant and was awarded the Distinguished Conduct Medal.

At this point, Gladys was working very long hours as a tram conductor. Throughout her time on the trams, she was on her feet as conductors were not allowed to sit even if the trams were empty. They were up and down the stairs in their long skirts - and the trams were open-top so upstairs was wet and cold in the winter. They were paid £1 (£95) a week, less if their takings did not tally with the number of tickets sold, because any shortfall was deducted. Depending on their shifts, she and her fellow female workers had to sign on at 7.30am and then could work until eleven or twelve at night, after which they had to make their own way home, through streets often without lighting - a wartime saving.

Gladys Wreford

At home, without doubt, Gladys would have been expected to give a hand, for her mother,

Mary, had younger children to care for: Constance, aged twelve, the twins, Willie and Herbert, aged five and two year old Sylvia. In all, Mary had given birth to thirteen children, of whom eight survived. It is to be hoped the family was as proud of their daughter, Gladys, as their hero son.

After the war, Gladys married William Diaper at St Paul's and gave up her work on the trams. A photograph of tram drivers and conductors taken in 1922 shows they were, again, all men. Gladys lived the rest of her life in the Corporation Road area, dying in 1989.

Before the war, 'clerks' were usually men but by the beginning of 1916, Newport Technical Institute had started classes to train women as quickly as possible to do all levels of office work. At a meeting of Newport Education Committee, it was said 'every trade and profession required them' and it was 'absolutely essential for Newport'. And not all these jobs were handed back to the men when they returned. The Post Office, banks and building societies especially valued women and kept them on.

The war also drained men from the land. There were constant appeals in the press for female farm workers. In Wales, women in rural areas were accustomed to working on the land, but with the men away, women from the towns were needed. The Women's Land Army was formed and vigorous recruitment ensued, in Newport as elsewhere. As the war progressed, food shortages caused anxiety and by 1917, women were even being urged to cultivate their gardens, especially for growing potatoes, which were being priced beyond the reach of the poor.

The upper and middle class women also played their part on the Home Front. They became charity collectors and organisers, becoming involved in areas in which they could assist the war effort. The following four chapters contain exemplary biographies, illustrative of the thousands of other Newport women who involved themselves in the war effort in so many of the diverse areas of life existing in the town at that time.

CHAPTER 13

Rosina Marion Cullimore

One such middle class woman was Rosina Cullimore. Her father, Ebenezer Evans, had been born in Newport but had settled in London long before Rosina was born in 1861.

Rosina Cullimore   © John's Who's Who in Newport 1920

He was a musician who made his living as a piano tuner and harp teacher. Rosina, too, was musically gifted. She grew up in Blooms-bury in a musical environment and when she was old enough, she was accepted as a student at the Royal Academy of Music, then located in Hanover Square, where she studied for six years, qualifying in piano, organ, singing and harmony. She became a teacher.

It is unclear when she moved to Newport but, at the time of the 1891 census, she was living at 9, York Place, Newport, as a boarder. As an Associate of the Royal Academy of Music, she was the local representative in the area and became involved with the musical life of the town. She continued to earn her living teaching until 23rd December 1896 when she married Alfred Millard Cullimore at St. Mary's Church, Newport. He came from a land-owning family of farmers from Llantarnam and Llanmartin and was a grain dealer. They set up home in 30, Ombersley Road and in 1899 their son, Donald, was born. Donald was about the same age as Violet Phillips whose grandfather lived at 28, Ombersley Road, so it is more than likely that they knew one another. The 1901 census shows the Culli-more family had one live-in servant.

In the summer of 1905, they had a daughter, Christina, and when Donald was old enough, he became a boarder at Llandaff Cathedral School in Cardiff. By the time of the 1911 census, they were living at Deepdene, 15, Fields Park Road. And so at the outbreak of war, the family were living a conventional, middle class life, but Rosina threw herself into war work.

She volunteered as a helper at the Uskside Munitions Works YMCA canteen, doing day and night duties for over a year, providing food for the workers. She later transferred to the YMCA Hut in Thomas Street, near the High Street Railway Station where she worked until after the armistice. The large huts were permanent camps provided by the YMCA in towns and cities, replacing the huge, temporary marquees erected by them early in the war. Each hut cost about £300 (£28,000), money which was raised through appeals and flag days in the locality. Money was also needed throughout the war to keep them supplied. On one occasion, a charity football match was played at Bailey Park in Abergavenny between Newport Ladies and Abergavenny Ladies to raise money for the YMCA huts. They were used to house, feed and give space for recreation and rest for troops stationed in the area and for the wounded.

YMCA headed notepaper

The provision of writing paper and pens was much appreciated by servicemen at home and abroad. The note paper carried the distinctive red triangular YMCA emblem.

Activities included film showings, dancing and concert parties. Music was a key part of the YMCA's wartime service. It had a music department which provided sheet music and instruments. Rosina's musical input must have been much appreciated. There were a number of these large huts in Newport, as well as the one sited at Newport Railway Station.

It was at the railway station that most Newport people got closest to the war. They gathered there to wave off sons and daughters, husbands, brothers and sisters who had joined the forces. They went back to see them return, many in ambulance trains. At the start, they were waved off with patriotic enthusiasm but as the reality of war sunk in and the years went by, the mood became more mixed.

The wounded, having been conveyed from the front in France to hospital ships, crossed the Channel and arrived at a British port. For those destined to come to Newport, this was usually Southampton. They were brought in ambulance trains to the railway station. In one particular week in July 1916, one hundred and thirty three wounded men were admitted to Woolaston Hospital on Saturday 8th, then on the following Thursday night, one hundred and eighty four more arrived at the station; on Friday the arrivals numbered three hundred and forty. Volunteers were informed of the arrival of trains by a notice in the window of the *Argus and Evening Post* premises opposite the station. Sometimes the management of the Olympia Cinema in Skinner Street would place notices on the cinema screen. From the station, the wounded were usually transferred to Woolaston Hospital by cars or vans. These vehicles were sent at a moment's notice from generous, private individuals like Gertrude Bailey and firms like Tovey's Funeral Directors. Occasionally trams were used but later in the war, there were ambulances. Rosina was a volunteer with the St. John's Ambulance Brigade and from September 1916 until the armistice, she met every single ambulance train which came to Newport, day and night, giving refreshments to nearly 20,000 wounded men.

Many concerts took place throughout the war in large concert venues like the Temperance Hall and also in church halls, hospitals and private homes, parks and gardens. They both raised money for war-related charities, and entertained the hundreds of wounded men from all the allied nations who were being cared for in the area. Rosina volunteered her musical services for the war effort. There was a large fund raising concert held on 15th February 1915, for instance, at which she was the accompanist. Over 500 soldiers were in the audience as well as many civilians. Another place where she performed was Beechwood Hospital, the sanatorium for service personnel and munitions workers with tuberculosis.

In addition to all of this she was an auxiliary worker at Woolaston Hospital.

Her son, Donald, trained as an engineer and after a period working for Great Western Railways, had joined the Artists Rifles. This was a regiment formed in 1859 and was made up of painters, sculptors, engravers, musicians, architects and actors. Some of its very earliest members were men belonging to the Pre-Raphaelite group of painters. During World War One, at the time Donald was serving with it, members included the painters Paul and John Nash, the poets Edward Thomas and Wilfred Owen, and playwright and musician, Noel Coward. They all served in the trenches and left their memories in their art. As Donald was educated at Llandaff Cathedral School, it is probable that he had inherited his mother's musical gifts. The Headquarters of the Artists Rifles was in St

Pancras, very near the home of his maternal grandparents who were then living in Hampstead. In 1917, Donald was commissioned as an officer in the Royal Flying Corps working in Farnborough and Winchester. He later returned to his unit. In October 1918, he was reported wounded. Later documentation shows he had suffered a gunshot wound to his right calf.

Despite what must have been constant anxiety about Donald, the war seems to have energised Rosina. Her entry in *Who's Who in Newport, 1920* states that the war led to a 'revival of her musical energies'. Prior to the war, married women were not allowed to be employed as teachers but the shortage of men meant married women were needed to fill the gaps. Records show that Rosina taught music at the Girls Intermediate School during the war. Indeed, one of her pupils there gained an open scholarship to the Royal College of Music and was awarded many medals and prizes for piano playing. Rosina was also one of the members of staff assisting at a school concert in Central Hall in May 1919. In that year, too, her name appears for the first time on the electoral register, one of the women then allowed to vote. The Representation of the People Act of 1918 allowed the vote to women over thirty for the first time.

After the war, she continued with her musical activities. Her entry in *John's Newport Directory* of 1929 is, 'Madam Rose Evans ARAM, Deepdene, is the Hon. Local Rep (Newport and Monmouthshire) of the Royal Academy of Music'. In the 1930s, she and her husband, Alfred, moved to Tenby where he died in 1942. Amazingly, Rosina lived to one hundred and four, dying in Newport in 1966.

CHAPTER 14

Mabel Annie Vivian

As a teacher at the Girls School, Rosina would have known another remarkable Newport woman who, although, like Rosina, not Newport-born, devoted her whole working life to the inhabitants of the town.

Mabel Annie Vivian was born early in 1870 in High Wycombe. Her father, who had come originally from Cornwall, was a civil servant working in the Inland Revenue. On the 1871 census, the family, consisting of Mabel, aged one, her parents, Edwin and Hannah, and her elder sister, Charlotte aged five, were living at Bicester Road, Aylesbury. They had two live-in servants, one of whom doubled up as a nurse.

Perhaps because of his professional advancement, the family moved around the country a number of times. At the time of the 1881 census, they were in Hastings.

In 1891 they were in Cardiff, living in Fitzalan Place. Both daughters had grown up and Charlotte had become a teacher in a private school. Mabel's entry reads, *'Student of Education BA/Training to be a teacher'*. Such a full description, taking two lines of script on the census form, suggests her parents were very proud of her accomplishments, as well they might be; she was exceptional.

Mabel studied at Cambridge Training College which had opened in 1885 specifically for training secondary school teachers. Throughout the nineteenth century, being a secondary school teacher was considered much more prestigious than an elementary school teacher. A degree in their subject was required, although it was only at the end of the century, when there was an expansion in secondary education requiring more teachers, that increasingly training colleges were set up. Cambridge University did not award degrees to women but trainees at the college could study for a degree at the same time. This meant an enormous workload. Mabel's degree was awarded by London University. She also spent some time as a student at University College, Cardiff.

An interesting point about her Cambridge days is that, while Mabel was at the training college, Millicent Fawcett's daughter, Philippa, was studying at Newnham College, Cambridge. The training college buildings were very near those of Newnham. It is more than possible that they met. Was this the start of Mabel's lifelong support for women's suffrage and particularly her involvement with the National Union of Women's Suffrage

Societies (NUWSS) headed by Millicent Fawcett? The organisation was democratic, aiming to achieve women's suffrage through peaceful and legal means, in particular by introducing Parliamentary Bills and holding meetings to explain and promote their aims.

Mabel's first post was in Norwich High School where she was an assistant mistress teaching classics from 1892 until 1895. Then she was appointed head of Newport Intermediate (later High) School for Girls. She took up her position on 1st January 1896, four months prior to the opening of the new school, to appoint staff and supervise the completion and fitting out of the building. She always praised Newport councillors for allowing her this valuable preparation time.

Mabel Vivian (seated centre) and her staff, not long after the school opened © *Jubilee Book*

Interestingly, her very first pupil, number one on the register, was Mary Yeomans, cousin of Violet Phillips. Mary later became a member of staff at the school. Its opening spelled the end for some of the private schools in the town. The girls' school was completely separate from the boys' school, the staff and pupils only coming together on special occasions. Many in the boys' school would not have agreed with some of Mabel's views. The boys' school's debating society in 1907 voiced stern disapproval of women's rights and equal opportunities.

In the 1901 census, she was living as a lodger in 45, York Place, near enough to the school on Queen's Hill to walk, although she was known to have been a cyclist. Newport's hills are not so cycle-friendly as the flat streets of Cardiff and Cambridge! The registers of 1906 show that Violet May Guy, younger sister of Nurse Alice Guy, was a pupil in Year Two. It would be so interesting to know if she ever spoke to Mabel about her sister. In 1911, Mabel was lodging at 9, Brynhyfryd Road. She appears to have also had a home in Cardiff. Her registration details with the Teachers Registration Council in August 1915 gives her address as 39, St Michael's Road, Llandaff. Her parents and sister had moved to Wilmslow in Cheshire by then.

In 1911, she became chair of the newly formed Newport branch of the National Union of Women's Suffrage Societies. Its members - suffragists, headed nationally by Millicent Fawcett - tried to achieve their aims politically through persuasion unlike the more radical Women's Social and Political Union. Both groups were united in their arguments against the Newport Branch of the National League for Opposing Women's Suffrage. Mabel missed no opportunity to encourage women to achieve equality. As a headmistress, she was in an ideal position to promote her views among her staff and pupils. An early member of staff, Irene Ashton-Jones, wrote many years later:

> *It was at Newport I first began to take an active part in public affairs. Miss Vivian who was the perfect chairman (I have never forgotten our Staff Meetings) stimulated the interest I already possessed in the Women's Movement and I left Newport to work for the enfranchisement of women.*

The *Weekly Argus* of 20th July 1912 states that Mabel was an invited guest at the Foundation Stone Laying Ceremony at Caerleon Training College earlier that week. She was presumably not pleased that it was to be a men-only college, the female training college to be sited at Barry. But maybe she had some silent sympathy with the suffragettes who had set fire to some building materials on the site the day before, protesting about the force-feeding of suffragette prisoners on hunger strike.

Also in 1912, on Wednesday 20th November, the VIP invited to present the prizes and certificates at the school's speech day was Margaret Mackworth, then at the height of her suffragette activity. In her address, Mabel remarked on the school's last, very pleasing inspection. Of the four members of the inspection team, she was delighted that, for the first time, half were women.

The *Weekly Argus* of Saturday, 19th July 1913 carried an article on Page 5, taking up five whole columns, entitled *Letter Box Firing Proceedings at Newport Police Court*. It was, of course, about the well-documented suffragette action by Margaret Mackworth and her resulting conviction. Further on in the same paper, on Page 9 and taking little more than two columns, was an article about a mass rally of the non-militant members of the Newport Women's Suffrage Society. Mabel Vivian, as chair of the society, with other members, met a party of about fifty 'pilgrims' from Cardiff Women's Suffrage Society and others from Blaenavon and Pontypool at the entrance to Belle Vue Park. They wore their suffragist colours of red, white and green, different from the suffragette colours of purple, white and green. Together, the suffragists processed to King's Hill Field to hear speakers argue for women's enfranchisement - but also to denounce lawbreaking as counterproductive. As a headmistress, Mabel could not endorse it, even for a cause so dear to her heart. But despite the fact that, nationally, the suffragists outnumbered the suffragettes, their actions were never as newsworthy.

The school was becoming highly successful. It admitted girls between the ages of ten and eighteen. They attended every weekday morning from nine until one. In 1914, the cost for each girl at the school was £3 (£320) a term, £2 10s (£260) for under twelves. In July 1914, just as the school holidays were about to start, Mabel received the good news that the plans for the longed-for extension and improvements, needed in the school, had been passed. But when war was declared a month later, the plans were put on hold and, in fact, were never started during her time as head. Mill Street Congregational Church Schoolroom was used to alleviate the lack of accommodation, which was hardly ideal.

In 1914, Mabel was living at 4, Dewsland Park Road. From August, the focus in the school

was very much on the war effort. In her recollections, Mabel describes the school going on a
huge knitting campaign. Everyone explored
ways to save and make money for the Soldiers'
Funds. Many economies were made, including
the girls forgoing their prizes on Speech Day
so that money could go to war funds. They
organised sales of donated items and their
own art work and knitted gifts. The girls and
staff wrote revues and performed them for the
wounded soldiers both at the school and at
Woolaston Hospital.

MISS M. A. VIVIAN, B.A., LONDON ; M.A., WALES (honoris causa)
FIRST HEADMISTRESS
1896 - 1931

A portrait of Mabel Vivian, taken from the school's Jubilee Book

At the school's Prize Day in November 1914, the guest invited to present the prizes was Gertrude Bailey. She 'heartily' congratulated Mabel Vivian on her report of the work of the school. The main speaker was Dr Winifred Cullis, a lecturer in physiology at the London School of Medicine for Women. She spoke encouragingly to the girls, telling them there was an enormous need for women doctors and they should consider training.

This was a subject of great interest to Mabel. At the meeting of 24th March 1915, at which Dr Elsie Inglis spoke about the Scottish Women's Hospital, Mabel Vivian spoke too, about her pride in women doctors and the need for more. Applicants had to be strong-willed and tenacious for there were enormous challenges. Medical schools did not welcome women, and hospitals would often not recruit them. The Royal Army Medical Corps flatly refused them and even the Red Cross disliked employing female doctors. By 1916, there was just one female doctor at the RGH, Charlotte Vines, employed as a civilian. Another woman doctor in Newport was Minna Benner who worked first as a schools medical officer and from 1917 in maternity and child welfare.

In fact, it took a very ambitious and determined woman to make it into any of the professions, and the greater the ambition, the harder it was. The doors of medicine had to be forced open, there were very few places for women lawyers and none for clerics. Most areas of academia discouraged women. In general, girls were not expected to be as well educated as their brothers. In order to educate the girls of Newport, Mabel had to fight hard against this prejudice, empowering girls to aim for the highest and not accept second best. She wanted this, not just for her pupils but for all the citizens of Newport and so during her time on Newport's Library Committee, she pushed for greater funding and more branch libraries.

When the war ended, Newport Education Committee granted the Intermediate School an extra week's holiday for Christmas. I would imagine this was greatly appreciated by Mabel as well as her staff and the girls.

In 1919, Mabel became eligible to vote. Her entry on the electoral register shows her living in her own home, 52, Llanthewy Road. In that year, the NUWSS became the National Union of Societies for Equal Citizenship (NUSEC), the very successful Newport branch of which she was to chair for many years. Margaret Mackworth was the national president.

This organisation stressed the importance of equality in areas such as the extension of the parliamentary franchise, equal pay, women police, birth control, divorce reform, and the removal of the marriage bar against women teachers, as well as maternity and child welfare. They promoted the welfare of women and children in the courts. They questioned parliamentary candidates on their views. The Representation of the People Act (Equal Franchise Act) 1928, which gave votes to women on the same terms as men at the age of twenty one, encouraged them to push for further measures to enhance women's equality in their public and private lives. They felt that equal citizenship was very different from equal voting rights.

Who's Who in Newport 1920 describes Mabel:

Member of the University Court (Wales) and the University Council of Music

Member of the Court of Governors and of the Council of University College, Cardiff and of Aberdare Hall, Cardiff (This latter was the female students' hall of residence.)

Member of the Executive Committee of the Central Welsh Board and of the Welsh County Schools Association

Member of the Newport Free Library Committee

President of Cardiff and District Association of University Women

She was awarded an honorary MA by Cardiff University.

In 1931, she retired to live in Cardiff and in 1946, she wrote: 'My life in Newport meant work, more and more work, but I would not have had it otherwise for it gave me lasting happiness'. She died in 1953.

CHAPTER 15

Gertrude Mary Bailey

Another woman, already mentioned and well known to Mabel Vivian, who also made an enormous contribution to the life of Newport, is described in *Who's Who in Newport 1920* as 'La Grande Dame' of Newport.

Gertrude Bailey   © John's Who's Who in Newport 1920

Gertrude Mary Buchanan was born in Sunderland, Durham in 1871, the eldest child in a large well-to-do family. She spent some of her very early years in Nova Scotia but most of her childhood was spent in a spacious house in Willow Bridge Road, Islington, London. Her father was a secretary to a shipping company and could afford to employ a cook, a nurse and housemaid.

On 20th March 1895, Gertrude married Charles Henry Bailey, a widower, originally from Tynemouth, Northumberland, who had set up a ship repair business in Newport in 1882: The Tyne Engineering Works. He had lived with his first wife, Charlotte, in Caerau Villa, Caerau Road, in Newport, and later Stelvio, a very large, beautiful house built for Charles just off the Bassaleg Road, Newport. This house was named after the ship on which he had arrived in Newport as chief engineer. Tragically, despite being listed by CADW, it was illegally demolished in 1996. There were no surviving children of Charles Bailey's first marriage.

With Gertrude, he settled in Stelvio and they started their family. By the time of the 1901 census, they had four children and also seven live-in servants: three nurses, two house-maids, a cook and a governess. Charles was a member of Victoria Road Congregational Church and a Freemason. CH Bailey, Ship Repairs, based in Newport Docks and Barry, was doing extremely well. Stelvio was filled with valuable antiques and artefacts as well as paintings by prestigious artists. An inventory of the jaw-dropping contents of the house, drawn up in 1920, is in Newport Reference Library. There were large formal gardens surrounding the house, including a large fishpond and an outdoor swimming pool.

Three more children were born to them before Charles' untimely death in 1907 of pneumonia. In all, they had five sons and two daughters: Charles Henry, James Nowell, George Buchanan, Gertrude Mary (Merriel), William Richardson, Edward Hardcastle and Elizabeth Metcalfe.

Charles' funeral was held in Newport on 15th February. There was a lengthy obituary in the *Argus*. Gertrude inherited the thriving business as well as all his property and effects, becoming a very wealthy woman. She purchased land at St Woolos cemetery for a family grave and monument.

After Charles' death, as well as taking over the management of the business, she concerned herself with her family and her interests, one of which was collecting inkwells. But she was also a philanthropist and threw herself into her role as one of Newport's benefactors. There were few areas of the life of Newport that she did not become involved with. She was a well-known public figure as well as one of the most successful businesswomen in the country. It was not easy for a woman to succeed in that male-orientated world of business and the fact that she did so reflects on her strength and energy.

By the time of the 1911 census, she was forty years old. Only two of her children were living at home: Charles, aged fifteen, and Elizabeth, aged four. She also had six live-in servants. All of her other children were away at boarding school: James and Edward in Weston-Super-Mare, George in Porthcawl and Gertrude (Merriel) at Cheltenham Ladies College.

She was the patron of the Newport and Monmouthshire Total Abstinence Society and the Band of Hope, actively supporting their events. On one occasion, she sent a letter of apology for not being able to attend a meeting of the Newport Branch of the National League for Opposing Women's Suffrage, which was particularly active in Newport in the years just prior to the outbreak of war. Whether her invitation to, and absence from, this meeting is significant, is difficult to tell. She was certainly willing to share platforms with Mabel Vivian, Margaret Mackworth and Sybil Thomas.

Prior to 1904, she had financed and run the only maternity training centre in Newport. The Maternity Nurses Home was situated at the junction of Cardiff Road and Herbert Street, opposite the Royal Gwent Hospital (RGH).

When this work was taken on by the authorities, she remained a member of the committee and a generous benefactor.

In 1911, to celebrate the coronation of George V and Queen Mary, she presented the town with the magnificent and costly mayoress's chain, believed to be one of the most valuable in the country.

The Mayoress' Chain, worn by Mayoress Jacqueline Mitchell September 2015

In 1912, in memory of her husband, she gave the Mortuary Chapel, with its beautiful stained glass window, to the Royal Gwent Hospital. She continued throughout her time in Newport to give generously to worthy causes. Twice in Mabel Vivian's Jubilee Book of 1946, she mentions large amounts of money being given to the school by Gertrude - on one occasion £200, which would be worth in excess of £8,000 today. A scholarship was funded and forty books were donated by her for the school library.

At the outbreak of war, she threw herself into numerous further activities to aid the war effort. The *Weekly Argus* of Saturday, 29th August 1914 has a headline, *Stitch! Stitch! Stitch!* for an article outlining in detail the large working parties of up to forty women which met in her house a few times a week to sew articles for hospitals and the poor. In 1912, she had been appointed president of the Newport and Monmouthshire (Royal Gwent) Hospital Needlework and Linen Guild, providing garments and linen for patients. After the outbreak of war, many of the patients were wounded and sick soldiers, Belgians at first, then later British and other allies, cared for at the hospital and The Friars Convalescent Home.

The same *Argus* article also mentions her involvement with the Red Cross Society to which she was also a generous benefactor, as well as the Belgian Relief Fund. Belgian refugees began to arrive in Monmouthshire in October 1914. By February 1915, five hundred and fifty had arrived through Newport and by the end of the year nearly eight hundred. Refugee committees were established in many parts of the county. There were fundraising appeals for wounded Belgian soldiers and Belgian refugee families.

In October 1915, she wrote a letter which was printed in the *Weekly Argus,* appealing for help to provide garments, linen, and so forth, for the Royal Gwent Hospital as at that time there were forty beds occupied by 'our gallant defenders' and another twenty planned. The first endowed bed at the hospital had been given by her in 1907, as requested in her late husband's will, but after the start of the war, she donated further beds.

She was a member of the Newport National Defence Committee which functioned partly as a recruiting agency. It decided to make over the Temperance Hall, one of the largest venues in Newport, for the recreation of members of the Armed Forces. She was chair of the Monmouthshire Prisoners of War Committee which supported Monmouthshire men who were captives in Germany. She also served on the local War Pensions Committee.

On 8th September 1917, a letter was printed in the *Weekly Argus* requesting readers' support to establish a crèche for the young children of munitions workers. It was written by the Lady Superintendent of the National

Cartridge and Box Factory, which at that time employed over two thousand women and was shortly to employ another three thousand. Some of the workers, she wrote, were comfortably off and did not need charity, but of particular concern to her were the number of mothers who needed to work to support their children. These women had no one to look after their children while they were in work. The factory hours were 6am to 5pm. The need for a crèche had been highlighted a few months previously at an education meeting that had been informed that children were missing school because they were needed to look after younger children while their mothers were at work. Gertrude pledged her support and was instrumental in organising and equipping the Newport Women Munitions Workers crèche. Pill Conservative Club at 50, Alexander Road, was converted at a cost of £250 (£26,000). Fundraising events were held including a football match at Somerton Park with teams drawn from the National Box Repairs Factory Ladies AFC. Gertrude guaranteed the wages of a nurse at the crèche which then allowed women with young children to work in the munitions factories. It was opened by her on 3rd December 1917.

There was hardly an edition of the *Argus* throughout the war which did not mention

The opening of the Munitions Crèche by Gertrude Bailey on 3rd December 1917

fund-raising events of various kinds. It printed lists of donors to war charities and the local hospitals, notifications of flag days and so on. Gertrude's acts of generosity are frequently mentioned. The workers of CH Bailey, too, contributed regularly. Throughout the war, the shipyards of CH Bailey were repairing and refitting warships and merchant ships.

Perhaps one fundraising event, organised by her for the Red Cross, should be mentioned. It was a 'treasure sale' which was opened by Sybil Thomas, by then Lady Rhondda, who made an impassioned speech about the work women were doing in the war and how, once the war ended, they would not go back to sitting at home. Then the bidding for valuable items started. At one point Gertrude and Sybil were bidding against one another for a Crown Derby inkstand. Gertrude bid seven guineas (£780) and won.

She showed particular acts of kindness in using her home, Stelvio, for charitable events. One 'At Home' in the summer of 1916 was for 'wounded soldiers, munitions girls and over a hundred visitors'. The one hundred and thirty munitions girls were employed at 'Messrs Bailey's works'. The wounded consisted of two hundred and fifty from Woolaston House, one hundred and twenty six from the Barracks and eleven from the Friars. There were professional musicians and entertainers and a programme of sports including boxing and a tug-of-war. The tea was provided in a marquee large enough for about seven hundred guests. Two of her sons were at home on leave on that occasion to assist her.

That same summer, she held a garden fête at Stelvio in which Rosina Cullimore was dressed up as a palm-reader sitting in a 'pagoda in the midst of a pool'. Maybe she used her professional name Madam Rose Evans for this!

All her sons except Edward, who was too young, joined the forces, so their safety must have been a constant worry. Every unexpected knock at the door must have brought acute anxiety; every letter a measure of relief.

Charles, who had had a radio station in Stelvio in the early days of radio and founded the Newport and South Wales Wireless Society, became an engineer and pilot. He served as a Captain in the Monmouthshire Regiment. James enlisted within weeks of the outbreak of war, being appointed Second Lieutenant 5th Huzzars and later Lieutenant in the 16/5th Lancers serving in France. William was a pilot, a Flight Lieutenant in the Royal Flying Corps.

She must have been particularly proud of her third son, Capt George Bailey, who was a Wing Commander in the RAF and was awarded the Distinguished Flying Cross for conspicuous bravery. During the battles of Canal du Nord and Cambrai, he flew very low over the enemy lines to inform the infantry of their position. He later became the chairman of CH Bailey. All survived the war, although a sister's son, Capt Charles Berjew Brooke DSO, aged twenty-one, died in the summer of 1916.

In June 1918, she was awarded the CBE. She was acknowledged as one of the most successful businesswomen in the country. The Sex Disqualification (Removal) Act was passed at the end of 1919, allowing women to become magistrates. In 1920, she became one of Newport's first two women magistrates, the other being Mrs MA Hart.

After 1920, she sold Stelvio, and its wonderful contents were auctioned. Some of its paintings she donated to Newport and they hang in the Civic Centre. Her business continued to flourish but, by then, her sons were involved too. She took to sailing the world and finally settled in Kenya with her younger daughter where she died in 1942.

CHAPTER 16

Mary Ann Hart

Mrs Mary Ann Hart was a woman from a very different background. She was born Mary Ann Williams in Bridgend in 1873 into a Welsh-speaking home. She was neither rich nor highly educated but she spent a life-time in public service.

Mary Ann Hart © John's Newport Encyclopaedia 1937

She moved to Newport, to 30, Capel Crescent, in Pill when she married Austin Jones in 1899. He was a railway guard for Great Western Railways (GWR). Mary was the local secretary of the Railway Women's Guild which was connected to the National Union of Railwaymen (NUR). This was a new, national organisation, formed to provide support to the wives and daughters of railway workers. It also sought to influence social and political issues. Particularly important topics of discussion amongst members were housing, full adult suffrage and pensions for men and women. They were founder members in 1906 of the Women's Labour League, a section of the Labour Party especially for women. At that time women were unable to join the main party but they raised money, supported Labour candidates and campaigned on women's issues.

By the time of the 1911 census, Austin and Mary were living at 72, Lewis Street in Pill. They later moved to number 67, now demolished, where Mary stayed for the rest of her life. They were both involved with the NUR Orphans Fund which raised money for food and clothes for the most needy. By this time, Austin had received promotion to Yard Inspector at work and was an active member of the Labour Party. By 1915 the NUR, of which Austin was an loyal member, was

admitting women members - an acknowlege-
ment of the huge number of women then
working on the railways, replacing men sent
abroad.

During the war, the Railway Women's Guild
championed women workers and women's
suffrage politically, and it was influential in
changing conditions for women and families.
The welfare of children was particularly
important. Early in the war, Mary attended a
meeting of the National Society for the
Prevention of Cruelty to Children (NSPCC) in
Newport, presenting a donation on behalf of
the Guild. In 1917, she was elected to the
organising committee of the Newport NSPCC.
There was much need. In just one month,
June 1917, it dealt with twenty-two cases
involving sixty children.

Of concern, especially after conscription of
single men between the ages of 18 and 41 in
January 1916, and married men of the same
age range in May 1916, were the dependants
of the men sent abroad. Without the main
wage earner, some families became destitute.
There was no welfare state and the poor relied
on charity. Mary worked as an investigator for
a charity providing support: the Soldiers' and
Sailors' Families Association (SSFA). This body
was asked by the Government to distribute
money, as necessary, from the National Relief

Fund which was money raised by charitable donations. A Separation Allowance was paid to the wives of married soldiers, their children and also any adults who could prove they were dependent on the soldier prior to his enlistment. This was not automatic but dependent on the local SSFA volunteer's decision regarding the worthiness of the recipient. Widows' Pensions also were not an automatic right. Recipients had to be of good character. Decisions were made locally by volunteers regarding the distribution of money, often, again, taking into account the class and moral standing of the recipients. There were many in Parliament who considered it unwise to give a lone woman money. There was a particular distrust of women in public houses. Cardiff imposed a curfew on women in the streets between 7pm and 8am which unfairly affected all ages and classes of women. In Newport, efforts were made to interpret the Home Office Order kindly. Each military wife had to register her details with the police but 'in the spirit of helpfulness', so that, if she became drunk, the police could take 'discreet and tactful action in order to prevent her from losing her separation allowance'.

Supporting such families must have heartbreaking work for Mary. She would have been very aware of the stigma they felt, receiving such payments as charity, and had to bear the resentment of those whose private lives were examined. The Women's Labour League lobbied Parliament to establish a fair, impartial system of allowances.

There was much poverty in Newport. She, and other members of the NUR and the Women's Guild, organised fundraising events for a widows and orphans fund. On one occasion described in the *Argus*, they held a flower show in the Gymnasium in Pill, in which Mary played an active part.

As in so many other places, Newport had concerns about the food shortage. Rising food prices led to demands for higher wages. As early as a few months into the war, there were press articles about increases in the price of bread and complaints from workers' organisations about the hardship this caused. The NUR was one of these, arguing that railwaymen had suspended their demand for better pay and conditions but were faced with higher prices because of those taking 'an unfair advantage of the present crisis'. Predictably, when shortages bit hard for the community, there were unscrupulous individuals who tried to make a quick profit. Also people began panic buying. As the war progressed, people were expected to ration their food voluntarily. Citizens were informed of their weekly allowance of bread, meat and sugar.

Food shortages and rationing would increasingly impact on people's daily lives. Prior to the conflict, Britain had relied on foreign imports for around 60% of its food, some coming from Germany and Austria. But the ruthless German strategy of using U-boats to target merchant ships resulted in an average of 300,000 tonnes of Britain-bound shipping being sunk every month, while a poor American harvest in 1916 served to exacerbate the situation. A slogan on a government poster urged people to 'Save the Wheat and Help the Fleet'.

By the autumn of 1916, the cost of basic food stuffs had risen enormously. The *Weekly Argus* of 16th September printed a table comparing prices in 1914 with those of 1916. A quarter of a pound of tea went from eight pence (£3.15) to a shilling (£4.70), a tin of milk from three and a half pence (£1.18) to seven pence (£2.75) and seven loaves of bread from two pound eleven pence (£193) to five pound and three pence (£473). For the poor, and those working with them like Mary, it must have been an anxious time.

Throughout all this time, also, there were hundreds of wounded and sick service personnel in the hospitals and convalescent homes in Newport, who required food. They relied on charitable donations. People who could, like Gertrude Bailey and other more fortunate citizens, donated food in large amounts for years.

By the middle of 1917, things were desperate for many. The press carried numerous articles about the quality and price of basic foodstuffs and carried many appeals for women to work on farms. There were war cookery columns with austerity recipes and practical advice for gardeners and allotment holders. The Rev Llewellyn-Jones announced he was going to hold Sunday services in allotments as that was where his parishioners were.

In July 1917, DA Thomas, Lord Rhondda, who had returned to the Government as the new Government Food Controller, ordered that certain food prices be fixed and the enforcing of this was delegated to the local food committees. Newport formed a Food Control Committee in August and Mary was asked to be a member. It met in offices at 23, Skinner Street. Its remit was to ensure people adhered to voluntary rationing and, where food was available to be purchased, that it was at a reasonable price. Shortages meant that grocery shops sometimes closed early as they had run out of stock. By the Christmas of 1917, the fourth Christmas of the war, austerity was biting hard and the food situation was high on everyone's agenda. It was estimated that the price of foodstuffs had increased by 110% since the start of the war. Potatoes and other basics were in short supply. Queues formed daily, even during the night, to buy what was available. The rich sent their servants to queue but the less well-off had to queue themselves. Women who were working sent their children. The Food Committee was very concerned about queuing and food hoarding. Those championing the poor and vulnerable, like Mary, called for statutory rationing.

In 1918, the Newport committee started controlling the supply of sugar, considered then to be a basic necessity. To ensure the poor were able to purchase their fair share, the price and distribution had to be regulated. Sugar cards were issued which were like a simple form of ration cards. When formal rationing of butter, margarine and tea was imposed in July 1918, the Newport committee decided to include meat as well, although this was frowned on by the government. The committee was the issuing body for the ration books and kept registers of who sold what, issued permits and monitored prices. This was not popular with food suppliers. There were numerous court cases for mis-selling food, for watering milk and for excessive charging.

And so throughout the war, Mary worked hard for fairness, kindness and equality for the citizens of Newport and when war ended, she was appointed to the Board of Guardians. As a tiny sign of change in the approach of male officialdom, her name in the appointment documentation was no longer Mrs Austin Jones but Mrs MA Jones. In 1919, she campaigned for Austin's successful election to the council, representing Tredegar Ward for the Labour Party. Also in 1919, the Railway Women's Guild supported the Newport Women's Citizen Association chaired by Mabel Vivian. In 1920, Mary became one of the first two women magistrates in Newport, the other being Gertrude Bailey.

Mary's Robing ceremony in the Council Chamber 9th November 1937. Her husband Harry Hart is second from the right
© *John's Newport Encyclopaedia 1937*

When Austin died in 1925, Mary stood for election in his place and became the first woman councillor in Newport. In 1937, she became its first woman mayor.

By this time, she had married widower Harry John Hart, another railway worker, and they continued to live in Lewis Street. At the National Eisteddfod of 1938 in Cardiff Castle, she was admitted to the Gorsedd and given the bardic title, Mair Gwelli, Mary of Pilgwenlly.

She retired from public life in 1954, having been granted the freedom of the borough and an OBE. She died in January 1961.

CHAPTER 17

The War's Legacy

There was a Victory Ball in the Westgate Hotel in January 1919, the WAACs, by then, having moved out. It was attended by Lord Tredegar, Gertrude Bailey and her two youngest children, and, amongst other dignitaries, Lewis Haslam. The latter had just been re-elected to Parliament to represent the new constituency of Newport in an election in which, for the first time, all men over twenty one and some women had been allowed to vote. That in itself was a sign of the changing times, as was the fact that, in much of the discussion prior to the election, commentators and politicians had to take into account the views of women and working class men. Although Lewis Haslam for the Liberal Coalition polled 14,080 votes, the Labour candidate, JW Bowen, was on his heels, polling 10,234. In Wales overall, Labour outvoted the Liberals for the first time.

By the end of the war, some of the divisions of class and gender within Newport were slowly breaking down. During the war, there had been much more social freedom. Age-old, invisible barriers had been crossed. People had pulled together, working towards a common goal. There had been a generosity of spirit. Was this permanent? Well, not all of it. Life, to some extent, returned to its pre-war grooves, although the death of so many men meant some women could not fulfil their traditional destiny of becoming wives and mothers. But the seeds of social change had been sown.

That may not have been immediately evident to some women. After demobilisation, the men who returned wanted their jobs back. Many had been protected by trades union agreements. The Restoration of Pre-War Practices Act of 1919 protected other jobs as part of the demand that everything was to return to pre-war conditions. There were criticisms of women who tried to hang on to a job. While they were working, women had been paying their National Insurance contribution so they were entitled to unemployment benefit, which was 25s (£80) a week. But this was only paid if no jobs were available and there was a demand for servants. So, for some single women, a forced return to domestic service was unavoidable, at least for a while. The marriage bar was reintroduced and would take decades to be removed again, forcing women back into their homes. Women's wages would take nearly a century to match those of men. Professional nurses, who had done amazing work, failed to get legal recognition of registered status until 1943. It would be the twenty-first century before Newport gained a female MP.

On the other hand, women had more freedom than they had had before the war. These were women who had been born in the Victorian era when upper class young women could not go out alone and respectable working class women were brought up strictly, having to be home in the evenings at a set time. In the war, they had been used to going out without being supervised. Many had moved away from home, away from their parents' jurisdiction, many had even gone abroad. Many had more money of their own. They cut their hair, they wore more comfortable clothes with shorter skirts. They now had experience of the workplace. They had shown they could equal men in the world of work and that experience could not be taken away. Additionally they were proud. They knew their work had allowed the war to be won.

On 10th August 1918, David Lloyd George, no longer in charge of munitions, having been made Prime Minister in December 1916, made a visit to Newport. Later, arguing in favour of women's suffrage, he wrote: 'My recent exper-ience in South Wales confirmed me in the conviction that the women there understand perfectly what is at stake in this war.' He praised 'the splendid manner in which the women came forward to work in hospitals, in munitions factories, on the land, in administrative offices of all kinds, and in war work behind the lines, often in danger of their lives...' The war would not have been won without them.

But no one forgot the terrible cost. It was a time of memorials. This war had been just so shocking, so terrible, that decisions were made that it should never be forgotten. There were huge memorials built in public spaces, in cities, towns and villages. Every church, club, school and workplace had their memorials. Rolls of honour were produced, with the compilers urging relatives and friends to inform them of casualties. Appeals were placed in the newspapers, including the *Argus*. Newport decided to give individual commemorative plaques to the next of kin.

Nationally, next-of-kin memorial plaques were issued to the bereaved families. They were nicknamed 'the dead man's penny', although they were issued for women casualties, too. Never before had ordinary service men and women been remembered in this public way. No one wanted to forget the sacrifices made by the men and women who gave their lives, and the injured, too, but also all the innumerable smaller, but hard, everyday sacrifices made by those on the home front and those sacrifices were mainly made by women. Ordinary women at an extraordinary time, they accepted the challenge of the times and rose to it.

The memorial plaque given to the next-of-kin of service personnel who died. This one is for Edward Bryant of Newport who was the great grandfather of Jayne Bryant, the present Assembly member for Newport West

All of the Newport women written about here should be remembered. Many were integral to Britain winning the war, yes, but they were more than that: they also paved the way for women coming later. When the war ended, women were out of the box. They had shown they were needed and were up to the challenge. They had done men's jobs. They had shown they were willing to pay the price like their hero brothers. Caroline Edwards, Lilian Jones, Alice Guy, Gertrude Dyer, Frances Llewellyn-Jones, Beatrice White and Violet Phillips, the women who died, daughters of Newport. And the women who did not die but paved the way for those of us who came after, women workers, women organisers, women in business, women who were highly educated, women who entered politics, women for peace, women who broke new ground and encouraged other women. They are part of Newport's rich heritage and should not be forgotten.

Bibliography

I have been researching off and on for about four years to gather the material used in this book. During this time, I have read a large number of books, newspapers and articles on websites. The following have been particularly helpful or deserving of mention:

Newport Teachers Great Roll of Honour 1923: *This is kept in Newport Reference Library*

The Welsh Book of Remembrance: *This is kept in the crypt of the specially built Temple of Peace in Cardiff. It has now been digitalised and is available online.*

John's Newport Directories, RH Johns Ltd, Newport

The Christmas Annual: Who's Who in Newport (1907/08) The Williams Press Ltd, Riverside Printing Works, Newport-on-Usk 1908

Who's Who In Newport 1920 RH Johns Ltd, Newport

South Wales Weekly Argus, with which are incorporated *South Wales Times and Star of Gwent, The Monmouthshire Merlin, Cardiff and Merthyr Guardian, Newport Gazette* and the *Chepstow Weekly Advertiser* 1912 - 1919

RC Slade *Newport Encyclopaedia, 1937*

Davis, Haydn (1988) *The History of the Borough of Newport,* Pennyfarthing Press

Underwood, Terry (1981) *The Way We Were in Newport* published by him

Knight, V Cliff and Jones, Alan V (2008) *Fifty Years*

of Newport 1900 - 1949 Oakwood Press

Ashwin, David (2009) *Newport Ghosts and the Great War 1914 - 1918*, Newport Printing Co

Roderick, Alan (1994) *The Newport Kaleidoscope,* Handpost Books

Dobbs Gary M (2015) *Cardiff and the Valleys in the Great War*, Pen & Sword Military 2015

Jones, Robin RGN, AICD (1988) *History of the Red Cross in Monmouthshire (Gwent) 1910 - 1918*, Red Cross, Gwent Branch

Peeling, Brian (2004) *The Royal Gwent and St Woolos Hospitals - A Century of Service in Newport.* Edited by Knight, Cliff, Old Bakehouse Publications

Report of Scottish Women's Hospital for Home and Foreign Service, Imperial War Museum, Department of Printed Books: Women's Work Collection. Ref: BRCS 24.6/3

Wallace, Ryland (2009) *The Women's Suffrage Movement in Wales 1866 - 1928*, Cardiff University of Wales Press

John, Angela V (2013) *Turning the Tide The Life of Lady Rhondda,* Parthian

Masson, Ursula (2010) *For Women, for Wales and for Liberalism, Women in Liberal Politics in Wales 1880-1914*, University of Wales Press

Bloxome, Marion *Women's Suffrage in Wales 1912 - 1914,* unpublished degree dissertation

Glover, EP *Newport High School for Boys The First Sixty Years 1896 - 1956*, (1957) RH Johns Ltd Newport

The Jubilee Book of the Newport High School for Girls 1896 - 1946 (1946) RH Johns Ltd Newport

Payne, Julian ed *Newport High School Magazine 1970s*

Richards, Derek (2002) *St Julian's Methodist Church Newport, Roll of Honour,* booklet

Adie, Kate (2013) *Fighting on the Home Front,* Hodder

Thomas, Gill (1989) *Life on All Fronts Women in the First World War,* Cambridge University Press

Stone, Jamie, *The Little Known Tragedy of HMS Natal,* The Northern Times, published on 08/11/2012

Hand-written records of PCC meetings and of baptisms and marriages, St John the Evangelist, Maindee, Newport

WEBSITES

Newport Past, *www.newportpast.com*

Newport's Dead, *www.newportsdead.shaunmaguire.co.uk*

Ancestry, *www.ancestry.com*

The Genealogist, *www.thegenealogist.co.uk*

Find My Past, *www.findmypast.co.uk*

Wikipedia, *www.wikipedia.org*

Commonwealth War Graves Commission, *www.cwgc.org*

British Red Cross, *www.redcross.org.uk*

General Records Office, *www.gro.gov.uk*

Women and War: Women's Archive of Wales, *www.womenandwar.wales*

Monmouthshire Baptisms and Marriages, *www.familysearch.org/search/collection*

Welsh Newspapers Online, *www.llgc.org.uk*

WalesOnline, *www.walesonline.co.uk*

HMS *Natal, www.hmsnatal.co.uk*

BBC *www.bbc.co.uk* report on 30/12/2015

BBC History, *www.bbc.co.uk/history*

Great War Forum, 1914-1918,
www.invisionzone.com

The Long Long Trail - The British Army in the
Great War of 1914-1918, *www.longlongtrail.co.uk*

Imperial War Museum, *www.iwm.org.uk*

Gwent Western Front Association,
www.gwentwfa.org.uk

The Merseyside Roll of Honour,
www.merseysiderollofhonour.co.uk

Forebears *www.forebears.co.uk*

Scarlet Finders *www.scarletfinders.co.uk*

The Peoples Collection Wales,
www.peoplescollection.wales

Scottish Women's Hospitals
www.scottishwomenshospital.co.uk

Forces War Records *www.forces-war-records.co.uk*

ABOUT THE AUTHOR

Sylvia was educated at Lady Margaret High School, Cardiff, The Western Theological College, Bristol and Bristol University where she gained a BA and a PGCE. While her son and daughter were young, she gained a Masters degree with the Open University, her specialism being Victorian poetry. Her career was spent as a teacher of English in secondary schools in Bristol, Newport and the Valleys.

Since retirement, having more time has meant being able to develop her interests in music, art history, literature, travel and embroidery. She particularly values the time she spends with her three lively granddaughters.

About the Publishers

Saron Publishers has been in existence for about ten years, producing niche magazines. Our first venture into books took place in 2016 when we published *The Meanderings of Bing* by Tim Harnden-Taylor. Further publications planned for 2017 include *Penthusiasm*, a collection of short stories and poems from Penthusiasts, a writing group based in the beautiful town of Usk, and *Frank,* a gentle novel about loss, by Julie Hamill.

Why not join our mailing list by emailing info@saronpublishers.co.uk. We promise no spam ever.

Visit our website saronpublishers.co.uk to keep up to date and to read reviews of what we've been reading and enjoying. You can also enjoy the occasional offer of a free Bing chapter.

Follow us on Facebook @saronpublishing.

Follow us on Twitter @saronpublishers.